"THE UNITED STATES finds itself impaled upon the horns of a dilemma. If it forces a peace upon Israel as the Arabs demand, it not only endangers Israel's survival but also incurs the wrath of millions of American Jews. If it supports Israel and supplies military hardware, then Americans run the risk of losing the friendship of the other industrialized nations who depend upon Arabs for oil, to say nothing of the consequences that an oil embargo would produce in the United States itself. More and more, the Arab world will pressure the U.S. to convince Israel to draw back from the occupied lands. More and More, the Arabs will force the U.S. and other oil-dependent countries of the West to support a new Palestinian state for the three million Arab refugees.

"Into such a complex situation as this will step the infamous antichrist. He will negotiate an Israeli withdrawal from the Arab territories. He will convince Israel that . . ."

Sanely, Biblically, and in contemporary language, John L. Benson dovetails current history with coming events in

THE SHOWDOWN
THAT WILL ROCK THE WORLD.

the Show-down

that will rock the world

John L. Benson

ACCENT BOOKS
Denver, Colorado

MEMBER OF
EVANGELICAL CHRISTIAN
PUBLISHERS ASSOCIATION

ACCENT BOOKS
12100 W. Sixth Avenue
P.O. Box 15337
Denver, Colorado 80215

Library of Congress Catalog Card Number: 77-79354

ISBN 0-916406-77-6

Contents

To the memory of
M.L. Lowe
esteemed Bible teacher
who first introduced me
to the system of
prophetic interpretation
in this book

1

The World Prepares for Antichrist

The World Prepares for Antichrist

The Mid East continues to be the political hotspot on planet earth. The threat of a renewed Arab-Israeli war keeps statesmen hopping in their frantic efforts to cool the hostile parties. No other place is more likely to become the scene of a military showdown that will rock the nations of the world to their very foundations. Every day brings the inevitable crisis nearer. It no longer belongs to the distant future; it looms on the horizon of history now.

Generations of Bible teachers have been telling us that civilization as we know it will meet its doom when the armies of the earth converge upon Palestine. Based on the writings of the prophets, they outlined in graphic detail the circumstances which would entice greedy peoples to plunder the resources of the Mid East. Not until the Mid East oil crisis, however, has anyone ever seen so clearly what makes the Mid East crucial to the Western world and what makes Israel such a prime factor in the debate over oil.

Here, in brief, is the situation. The whole Arab world and the State of Israel live today in a temporary interlude from war which is dependent upon periodic extensions of a fragile truce and upon the presence of United Nations' peace-keeping forces. The Arabs maintain that the Jewish state has no right to exist in Palestine. Especially are the Arabs insistent that Israel withdraw from the territories which she conquered in the Six-Day War of 1967.

The Israelis contend that they are a sovereign state, legally established as such by the United Nations in 1948 and at that time fully recognized by the superpowers. The Israelis refuse to surrender the occupied lands because they are indispensable to Israel's defense. The initiation of permanent peace in the Mid East requires that Israel withdraw from the Golan Heights, the left bank of the Jordan River, the old city of Jerusalem, and the Sinai Peninsula. Arabs declare that no other alternative is acceptable. The Israelis believe that such a unilateral withdrawal is nothing short of national suicide.

Until 1973 the opposing forces stood at a stalemate. Then in October of that year the Arabs launched a sneak attack upon Israel while the Jews were observing the Yom Kippur celebration in their synagogues. The Arabs enjoyed early successes. Jewish casualties were enormous. The Arabs demonstrated a new efficiency and a new unity. The fortunes of war, however, soon turned in Israel's favor. Israeli armies crossed the Suez Canal and penetrated deep into Egypt. On the eastern front the Israeli forces advanced to within striking distance of Damascus. As soon as the Syrians and the Egyptians went on the defensive, Russia called for a cease fire which prevented Israel from scoring a decisive victory.

The Yom Kippur War of 1973 has made world politicians acutely conscious that the Mid East situation affects the whole earth. That war introduced a new Arab unity, and out of it has come a new Arab strategy. The Arabs have shifted from reliance upon Russian military assistance to a plan to blackmail the Western nations into withdrawing support from Israel. The new diplomacy consists of an oil embargo. The Arabs nationalized foreign oil companies with the result that a few leaders now control most of the world's petroleum reserves. By nationalization the Arabs came into possession of the most advanced production and processing equipment. Overnight the price of oil shot up from $1 a barrel to as high as $17 a barrel. This tactic is draining the Western world of its financial assets. Arab nations now have the capital for astronomical investments and lending. The Mid East has become a major factor in every international consideration. The Mid East is in a position to dominate the world.

The United States of America has unofficially commited

itself to defend Israel. In July of 1977 rumors circulated that the U.S. was even considering the advisability of developing a military base in Israel. The U.S., on the other hand, cannot afford to alienate the Arabs. American economy cannot survive without Arab oil. Americans depend upon millions of barrels of Mid East oil every day. They fear the escalation of oil prices with its attendant inflation. They shudder to think of what would happen if the oil-rich nations should shut off the supply altogether. Western industry would grind to a halt.

The United States finds itself impaled upon the horns of a dilemma. If it forces a peace upon Israel as the Arabs demand, it not only endangers Israel's survival but also incurs the wrath of millions of American Jews. If it supports Israel and supplies military hardware, then Americans run the risk of losing the friendship of the other industrialized nations who depend upon Arabs for oil, to say nothing of the consequences that an oil embargo would produce in the United States itself. More and more, the Arab world will pressure the U.S. to convince Israel to draw back from the occupied lands. More and more, the Arabs will force the U.S. and other oil-dependent countries of the West to support a new Palestinian state for the three million Arab refugees.

Into such a complex situation as this will step the infamous antichrist. He will negotiate an Israeli withdrawal from the Arab territories. He will convince Israel that she can do so in perfect safety, for the Western allies will have signed a treaty with Israel which guarantees the inviolability of Israeli borders and promises to defend Israel from aggressors. Some Israelis will argue against such an alliance; they will warn the nation that they must depend upon their own defenses and not trust other nations to secure them. The majority, however, will listen to the persuasive oratory of their prime minister and follow his plan for a permanent peace. He may internationalize the Temple area. He will probably bring about a complete disarmament. The development of these events is the subject of chapters 2-6 in this book.

The peace settlement will eventually take the nations of the world to Armageddon. The Arabs on the southern border of Israel will violate the peace agreement by invading Israel. They will determine to control the Mid East. Such audacity and greed will bring the Russian armies down from the north to frustrate Arab designs. In the process the Mid East will undergo an unprecedented military bloodbath. The presence of the Russian armies in the Mid East will motivate Israel's Western allies to come to Israel's defense, in accord with treaty stipulations. The determination of the Western powers to control the wealth of the Mid East will stir up the jealousy of Oriental countries in the Far East. These will swarm into Palestine. The result is Armageddon, and chapters 7-10 discuss the grim details of all these events.

Armageddon spells the doom of civilization as we know it; it does not mean, however, the end of the world. It means only the end of a long period in history during which the Gentile powers have held political mastery. The awesome destruction of life and property which accompanies the mobilization of world armies will conclude an epoch in history and prepare the way for the dawn of a new age in which the Lord Jesus Christ will personally preside as King of nations and as Lord of history. He will permanently solve the Mid East problem and maintain peace. These are the events which will occur after Armageddon, and they are the subject of chapters 11-14.

Antichrist, Armageddon, and after — under these terms fall most of the major themes of Biblical prophecy. The person who understands what the Scriptures say about these truths and who sees the implications of these things is the person who best discerns the momentous times in which we live. Biblical prophecy illumines current events as nothing else can. It assures the Christian that history is an intricate plan and moves toward a purposeful conclusion under the management of the King of kings and the Lord of lords.

THE SHOWDOWN . . .

2

The Coming of
the Counterfeit Christ

The Coming of the Counterfeit Christ

Who really is the antichrist? Can we know? Is he a person or a philosophy? Is he a Jew or a Gentile? Is he a political or a religious figure? Does he exercise military or economic power? Is he a prophet, a king, or a priest? Is he a man or a devil? What part of the world will he dominate? Is he alive today?

Christians have always had a tendency to identify the antichrist with every wicked leader that steps onto the stage of history and figures in world crises. In ancient times believers thought that Nero was the antichrist. The Protestant Reformers with almost no dissenting voice regarded the pope as the antichrist. They believed it was not any one particular pope but a whole succession of popes.

In more recent times Napoleon was nominated to the position of the antichrist. Kaiser Wilhelm of Germany became a likely candidate for this post. Later, both Hitler and Mussolini looked like good prospects. While Henry Kissinger was shooting back and forth across the Middle East like a blazing comet, bugs on prophecy were sure he was the antichrist. Now that he is no longer Secretary of State, prophetic interest in him has subsided.

We must seek out the answers to these questions from the only source that can give us an authoritative reply—the Bible.

In the entire Bible the word "antichrist" occurs only five times, and the epistles of John contain all of these references. This is the most logical place, then, for us to begin our investigation.

The first mention of antichrist is in I John 2:18:

"Little children, it is the last time: and as ye have heard that antichrist shall come, even now are there many antichrists; whereby we know that it is the last time."

A certain indication of the soon return of Christ to the earth is the coming of the antichrist. And the Apostle John's "little children" had received plenty of instruction about the antichrist. The information was already widespread at the time John wrote his epistle, late in the first century. John was not telling believers anything new. They associated the coming of the antichrist with the "last time." They concluded that because the antichrist had not yet appeared, they were not yet living in the last time.

The aged apostle wished to correct this view. He declared that his readers were already living in the last time, or, literally, the last hour. Indeed, *the last time really includes the whole period between the first and second advents of Christ,* no matter how long or short this period turned out to be.

John explained that his little children did not have to wait until the antichrist arrived in order for them to realize they were living in the last time. The very fact that "many antichrists" were already at work in the church was sufficient proof that the return of Christ for His church was imminent. All indications pointed to the fact that the church age was about to come to a close.

What is the significance of antichrist and many antichrists? Some Bible teachers believe these references point mainly to a system or philosophy that prevails in the last days. They see antichrist not as one person but as any person who teaches false doctrine.

As far as it goes, this position is correct. Of course, all false teachers from the time of the apostles to the present are antichrists. But this does not rule out the possibility of one final, personal, individual antichrist. In fact, the famous Greek scholar B. F. Westcott says that "the absence of the definite article ('the') shows that ('antichrist') had become current as a technical (proper) name."

The truth of the matter is that the "many antichrists" who arise all during the church age will culminate in a final person. The many antichrists are forerunners of the personal antichrist. The forerunners believe and teach the same things that the antichrist will eventually believe and teach.

Notice in I John 2:19 that antichrists are apostates:

> "They went out from us, but they were not of us; for if they had been of us, they would no doubt have continued with us: but they went out, that they might be made manifest that they were not all of us."

At one time these apostates identified themselves with some local church. From all outward appearances they seemed to be genuine Christians. But the time came when they renounced the distinct truths of Christianity. By departing from Biblical truth, they demonstrated that they had never really become Christians at all.

They had never received "an unction from the Holy One," and so they were ultimately incapable of continuing in the truth or even of knowing the truth (I John 2:20). Only genuine Christians have an unction from the Spirit which enables them to discern the truth, teach the truth, and persevere in the truth.

Antichrists are all apostates. The personal antichrist will be the final apostate. He will be the personal embodiment of religious error and falsification of the Biblical truth. Verse 22 emphasizes this point:

> "Who is a liar but he that denieth that Jesus is the Christ? He is antichrist, that denieth the Father and the Son."

In the Greek text the word "the" precedes "liar" and also

precedes "antichrist." John actually wrote about *the* liar and *the* antichrist.

The antichrist is *the* liar. He is the personal embodiment of all the lies that ever circulated about the Lord Jesus Christ. All of the predecessors of the antichrist have sought to refute the claims of Christ to be the Messiah, but the antichrist will surpass them all. The antichrist will actually pose as the Messiah; he will claim Messianic titles and privileges.

The antichrist is essentially a counterfeit christ, a fact which the text in I John 2:18,22 supports. The Greek word for "antichrist" is *antichristos;* it is composed of *anti* (meaning "in stead of") and *christos* (meaning "anointed one"). Antichrist, then, refers to a substitute christ, an imitation christ, a rival christ. The antichrist is a person who will attempt to convince Israel that he is their long-anticipated Messiah.

Westcott says that the antichrist is "one who takes the place of Christ." He concludes that "one who assumes the guise of Christ opposes Christ." In other words, the antichrist opposes Christ in the sense that he poses as Christ and passes himself off as being Christ. In the main, he is a fraud, a fake, and a false christ. Greek grammarians H. E. Dana and J. R. Mantey concur with Westcott's explanation of *anti:* "There is conclusive proof now that the dominant meaning for *anti* in the first century was *instead of.*"

Like the many antichrists who prepare the way for him the final antichrist will contradict the truth. The Father has identified Jesus of Nazareth as the Messiah. The antichrist will say, "No, I am the Messiah." By denying that Jesus is the Messiah the antichrist will deny that the Father tells the truth.

Also, like his predecessors, the antichrist will tell lies in order to seduce people:

> "These things have I written unto you concerning them that seduce you" (I John 2:26).

THE SHOWDOWN . . .

Antichrists and *the* antichrist cause people to stray away from the real truth about the Lord Jesus Christ.

In chapter four of I John, the apostle mentions "antichrist" for the fourth time. The context still has to do with truth and error. In verse 1, John warns his "beloved" children not to believe everything they hear which has a religious overtone. He instructs them to examine carefully the doctrines they hear. With spiritual discernment they can decide whether the teaching originates from God or from man, whether it is the absolute truth or contaminated with error.

Interestingly enough, John warns believers not about false teachers but about false prophets.

> "Beloved, believe not every spirit, but try the spirits whether they are of God: because many false prophets are gone out into the world" (verse 1).

In the first century, prophets still functioned (Acts 13:1; 21:9,10). As the result of special and direct revelation from God, the prophet gave divine utterances. In order to convince hearers that their utterances carried divine authority, the prophet performed miraculous deeds (I Corinthians 12:10). The miracles authenticated the prophet's message. A teacher only imparted and explained the truth; a prophet received new truth directly from God and performed miracles in order to corroborate the fact that his message had indeed come directly from God's mind to his mind.

Just as the many antichrists of I John 2:18 are the equivalent of the many false prophets of I John 4:1, so the antichrist of I John 2:18 in all probability is the false prophet of Revelation 19:20:

> "And the beast was taken, and with him the false prophet that wrought miracles before him, with which he deceived them that had received the mark of the beast, and them that worshipped his image.

These both were cast alive into a lake of fire burning with brimstone."

The Apostle John singles out, in I John 4, one enormous falsehood which false prophets were then spreading about the Lord Jesus Christ. They said that Jesus Christ was not God incarnate (verse 2). They denied that the Word became flesh and dwelt among us. This doctrinal error is antichristian—it is the spirit of antichrist (verse 3). The spirit of antichrist is the spirit of error (verse 6). The error is strictly doctrinal. John has heresy in view whenever he refers to antichrist.

The fifth reference to antichrist occurs in II John, verse 7:

"For many deceivers are entered into the world, who confess not that Jesus Christ is come in the flesh. This is a deceiver and an antichrist."

Here again, John speaks of many deceivers and, literally, *the* deceiver, not "a deceiver." The many deceivers are only the predecessors of the arch deceiver, just as the many antichrists are only the predecessors of the final personal antichrist and the many false prophets are forerunners of the final false prophet.

The deception once more involves a theological matter. John is referring to a special breed of deceivers; namely, those deceivers who will not acknowledge that Jesus is God incarnate. The person who will carry this deception to the ultimate is the antichrist.

The use of the definite article "the" before the words "deceiver" and "antichrist" makes a rather strong argument for a personal antichrist. It indicates that he is going to be a well-known figure, someone who has often been the subject of discussion.

What have we, therefore, learned about the antichrist? (1) He is a person. (2) He will come before the Lord's return to earth—that is, "in the last time." (3) He is a substitute christ. (4) He is *the* liar of all time. (5) He is an apostate of some sort. (6) He contradicts religious truth and especially deals in religious matters. (7) He is a seducer. (8) He is associated with the spirit of error. (9) He is *the* deceiver. (10) He is the culmination of all the antichrists and the false prophets who precede him. His forerunners are deceivers, antichrists, and false prophets. We may, therefore, reasonably expect that if he is *the* deceiver and *the* antichrist, he is also *the* false prophet.

3

A Description of the World's Biggest Liar

A Description of the World's Biggest Liar

Gradually the Biblical picture of the antichrist is materializing before our eyes. The Apostle John, in his first two epistles, says the antichrist will come, that he will be *the* deceiver, that he will be involved in apostasy, that he will oppose Christ in the sense that he poses as Christ, and that the spirit of antichrist is already at work.

Now, is there any other passage in the Bible that contains all of this information about a wicked end-time leader? We do not have far to look for an answer. The Apostle Paul repeats this data in detail in his second letter to the Thessalonians, and adds a few more touches to the emerging figure of the antichrist.

The Apostle John had to correct his people because they thought the last times would not come until the antichrist arrived. The Apostle Paul had to correct the Thessalonians because they thought they were living in the dreaded tribulation period—the day of the Lord.

John explained that you can recognize the last times by the activity of many antichrists. Paul explained that you can recognize the day of the Lord by the revelation of the man of sin:

> "Let no man deceive you by any means: for that day shall not come, except there come a falling away first, and that man of sin be revealed, the son of perdition" (II Thessalonians 2:3).

Paul argued that the man of sin had not yet appeared, and so the day of the Lord had not come either. The persecutions which the Thessalonians suffered were no proof at all that the day of the Lord's wrath was already in progress. Paul told the Thessalonians that *the* apostasy ("a falling away") had not come yet, and the man of sin had not arrived yet. The presence of these two events would indicate the introduction of the period of God's wrath.

Having relieved the minds of the Thessalonians, Paul proceeded to describe the man of sin and the day of the apostasy. Jesus Christ is the Son of man (Matthew 17:9) and the man of sorrows (Isaiah 53:3). By contrast, the wicked leader of whom Paul speaks here is the man of sin. He is the personification and embodiment of sin, just as the antichrist is the embodiment of lies. He is the man in whom sin culminates. Sin absolutely and unqualifiedly dominates him. Christ is just the opposite. He is the man without sin. In Him is no sin (II Corinthians 5:21). He is the essence of holiness.

The man of sin will have a "revelation"—that is, a denouement, a disclosure. In this he imitates Christ, who also will be revealed (I Peter 1:13). The man of sin is the son of perdition. Perdition indicates his destiny, not necessarily his origin. Sin will lead him to ruin.

Some Bible teachers believe that the man of sin will be Judas raised from the dead. They base this view on the fact that Jesus called Judas "the son of perdition" (John 17:12). This does not prove that Judas is the son of perdition whom Paul describes here. The most we can infer is that Judas and the man of sin are both ruined men and appointed to perdition. Both Judas and the man of sin, of course, are controlled by the devil. They have perhaps much in common, but they are not one and the same man.

The man of sin will be a cheap imitation. Notice that in II Thessalonians 2:4 we have an exact parallel with the description of antichrist in the epistles of John:

"Who opposeth and exalteth himself above all that is called God, or that is worshipped, so that he as God sitteth in the temple of God, shewing himself that he is God."

THE SHOWDOWN . . .

The man of sin opposes not by denying the existence of God but by posing as God in the temple of God.

The man of sin claims divine honors. He deifies himself. By occupying a place in the temple, he assumes the role of a priest. In two respects he imitates Christ: (1) by claiming divine titles and honors; (2) by professing to be a priest. When the Messiah finally reveals Himself, He will sit as a priest upon His throne in the temple at Jerusalem (Zechariah 6:13).

Just as John's people had heard all about antichrist before, so the Thessalonians had heard all about the man of sin before:

> "Remember ye not, that, when I was yet with you,
> I told you these things? And now ye know what
> withholdeth . . ." (II Thessalonians 2:5,6).

Just as many antichrists were working prior to the coming of the personal antichrist, so the mystery of iniquity was working prior to the revelation of the man of sin:

> "For the mystery of iniquity doth already work"
> (verse 7).

The word "iniquity" in this verse is literally "lawlessness." The words "wicked [one]" in verse 8 are literally "lawless one." Lawlessness will precede the lawless one, just as antichristian activities precede the antichrist himself.

The man of sin will have not only a revelation but also a "coming":

> "And then shall that wicked one be revealed, whom
> the Lord shall destroy with the spirit of his mouth,
> and shall destroy with the brightness of his coming:
> even him whose coming is after the working of
> Satan with all power and signs and lying wonders"
> (II Thessalonians 2:8,9).

"Revelation" is the Greek word *apocalypsis;* "coming" is the Greek word *parousia.* The man of sin will imitate Christ whose return is described as both a revelation and a coming, an *apocalypsis* and a *parousia.*

The man of sin will have supernatural powers. Both the Christian and the Christ have an anointing; we have an unction from the Holy Spirit (I John 2:20). The man of sin and all of his evil forerunners, on the other hand, work under the influence of Satan.

Jesus received the Spirit's ministry without measure (John 3:34). He was anointed with the oil of gladness above His fellows (Hebrews 1:9). He performed His miracles in the power of the Holy Spirit.

The man of sin will also depend upon a supernatural strengthening and control. The devil will energize him and enable him to perform a variety of miracles: "power and signs and lying wonders" (II Thessalonians 2:9).

Jesus performed miracles in order to authenticate His prophetic credentials. God had promised to raise up a prophet like Moses (Deuteronomy 18:18). Jesus was that prophet, and He proved it by His miraculous works.

When the counterfeit christ arrives, he will perform miracles in order to convince Israel that he is the prophet like Moses. The man of sin sits as a priest in the temple and engages in a prophetic ministry.

The miracles which the man of sin performs are counterfeit, like the miracles of the pharaoh's magicians who tried to duplicate Moses' miracles (Exodus 7:8-13; II Timothy 3:8). They are "lying" wonders. The man of sin cannot really perform miracles, but he will convince his followers that he can. He will win their devotion through deceit, trickery, and fraud. He will appeal to people who are easily deceived. They are easily deceived because they are unrighteous. These unrighteous people will believe *the* lie:

"And with all deceivableness of unrighteousness
in them that perish; because they received not
the love of the truth, that they might be saved.

25

> And for this cause God shall send them strong
> delusion, that they should believe a lie" (II Thessa-
> lonians 2:10,11).

The whole deception pertains to "the love of the truth."
The deception involves religious and spiritual realities.

In establishing an identity for the antichrist, the correla-
tion between II Thessalonians and the references to antichrist in the epistles of John is too plain to miss. Both John
and Paul speak about opposition (John uses the prefix
anti). Both mention the previous knowledge of their hearers.
Both describe the conditions that precede the antichrist.
Both refer to deceit and to lies. Both treat the subject of
Biblical truth. Nothing can be more certain than that the
antichrist of I and II John is identical to the man of sin, son
of perdition, and that lawless one in II Thessalonians
chapter two.

Paul, however, adds some information which John does
not include. Paul explains that the man of sin will perform
miracles in order to deceive those who perish (II Thessalonians 2:9,10). The man of sin is a miracle-worker and a
religious deceiver. When we hunt for such a person in the
book of Revelation, we are not long in spotting him. The
miracle worker and religious deceiver is described in
Revelation 13:11-18.

Nothing we have learned about the antichrist in I and II
John or in II Thessalonians fits the description of the first
beast in Revelation 13:1-10, whom many persons claim is
the antichrist. The first beast is definitely a political figure,
as all Bible students readily acknowledge. The first beast
never performs a miracle and never claims to be Christ, the
prophet-priest.

The second beast is *the* religious figure of the "day of the
Lord." This beast, beast out of the earth, is the man of sin
and the antichrist. This beast out of the earth imitates
Christ in everything that he says and does. Revelation
13:11-18 shows how the second beast poses as Christ. He is
a lamb-like figure:

> "And I beheld another beast coming up out of the
> earth; and he had two horns like a lamb, and he
> spake as a dragon" (verse 11).

The Lord Jesus is the lamb of God who took away the sin
of the world (John 1:29). The lamb belongs to the Old
Testament sacrificial system. It is a religious emblem. The
two horns of verse 11 suggest power or authority.

The true nature of the beast out of the earth comes to light
when he speaks; he sounds like a dragon. Of course, Satan
is the dragon, and Satan empowers this religious leader to
sway the multitudes with his oratorical genius. He is
Satanically motivated and activated (Revelation 13:13,14).

The beast out of the earth is categorically NOT inferior to
the beast out of the sea. The second beast "exerciseth all the
power of the first beast" (Revelation 13:12). The religious
leader is equal in authority to the political leader. He
exercises the same authority in the religious sphere that the
first beast exercises in the political sphere. In this the
second beast imitates Christ, who claimed equality with the
Father (John 5:18).

The beast out of the earth, the antichrist, is responsible
for making the first beast an object of worship. He deifies
the political leader and enforces the worship (Revelation
13:12). This does not mean, however, that the second beast
refuses worship for himself. The second beast will sit in the
temple at Jerusalem, showing that he is God. In this he
copies Christ, for Jesus not only directed worship to the
Father but received worship for Himself (Matthew 4:10;
28:17). Both the political leader and the religious leader of
the end-time will claim divine honors.

The second beast's involvement in worship suggests that
he functions as a priest. His miraculous powers suggest
that he functions as a prophet:

> "And he doeth great wonders, so that he maketh
> fire come down from heaven on the earth in the
> sight of men" (Revelation 13:13).

27

John and Paul agree that the antichrist is a prophet-priest. Paul says he works "all power and signs and lying wonders." John says "he doeth great wonders."

The antichrist knows that Jews expect their Messiah to come in the style of Elijah, who called down fire to destroy God's enemies (Malachi 4:5). The antichrist will perform this feat to the amazement of spectators. They will be convinced by spectacular evidences that the second beast is the Messiah.

John names the antichrist as a deceiver (II John 7). Paul makes deceit a prominent characteristic of the man of sin. Now Revelation 13:14 applies this deceit to the second beast, not to the first beast:

> "And deceiveth them that dwell on the earth by the
> means of those miracles which he had power to do
> in the sight of the [first] beast."

The first beast is neither the deceiver nor the antichrist. The first beast is a Gentile dictator who presides over the Western division of the coming reorganized Roman empire. The Western dictator (sometimes called the Roman prince) is a colleague of the antichrist; together, they are co-rulers over the coming empire of the Caesars.

In some ways the second beast is, by far the worse of the two. He is an imposter. He pretends to tell the truth, but all the while he is lying through his teeth. He is responsible for the damnation of perhaps millions. By distorting and destroying the truth, he will control the minds of his subjects.

In the middle of the tribulation period, the Roman prince will assume dictatorial power (Revelation 17:12,13). He will destroy the ecumenical church (Revelation 17:16). He will depend upon the antichrist then to promote emperor worship. The antichrist will gladly comply with the emperor's desire to have a statue of the emperor erected in the rebuilt temple in Jerusalem. The antichrist will place this image in the holy of holies (Matthew 24:15). The antichrist will use his trickery to make people think the statue has come alive:

> "Saying to them that dwell on the earth, that they
> should make an image to the beast, which had the
> wound by the sword and did live. And he had power
> to give life unto the image of the beast" (Revela-
> tion 13:14,15).

When the statue speaks, the crowds will prostrate themselves before it in an act of worship. Those who dissent will
be destroyed. The antichrist in a fit of rage will "cause that
as many as would not worship the image of the beast
should be killed" (verse 15). By giving life (literally,
"breath") to the image, the antichrist will once more pose
as Christ, for Jesus restored life by His miraculous powers.

When the antichrist comes, people will know economic
controls such as have never been dreamed of before. The
second beast of Revelation 13 (the antichrist) is more than
just a religious leader who claims to be Israel's Messiah. He
is a commercial and economic leader who has the power to
feed the people or starve them, just as he pleases:

> "And he causeth all, both small and great, rich and
> poor, free and bond, to receive a mark in their right
> hand, or in their foreheads: And that no man might
> buy or sell, save he that had the mark, or the name
> of the beast, or the number of his name" (Revela-
> tion 13:16,17).

He will so control commerce that no one can buy or sell
anything unless he has a mark which identifies him as a
beast worshiper. Just as Christ fed the multitude who
followed Him, so the antichrist will feed the masses who
follow him. The two horns of the second beast suggest the
dual authority of the man of sin—authority in religion and
also in economy.

In all likelihood the antichrist will establish his religious
capital at Jerusalem and his commercial capital at rebuilt

THE SHOWDOWN . . .

Babylon on the Euphrates River (Zechariah 5:5-11). He will control the Eastern division of the reorganized Roman empire. All together, the Roman empire will extend from the Atlantic seaboard of Europe to the Persian Gulf. Especially will the lands of the Mediterranean Sea figure prominently in the end-time crisis.

We have all heard about the mark which the antichrist will give. Please note that the second beast gives this mark, not the first beast. We have also all heard about the enigma of the number 666:

> "Here is wisdom. Let him that hath understanding count the number of the beast: for it is the number of a man, and his number is six hundred three-score and six" (Revelation 13:18).

It is the number of a man. We cannot help thinking of the man of sin, for the second beast and the man of sin are the same person.

The number 666 occurs in only one other place in the Bible. Ezra 2:13 says that the descendants of Adonikam numbered 666. "Adonikam" means "the king who rises up." Perhaps when the beast arises out of the earth, he will actually be called Adonikam. By his name and his deeds the tribulation saints will immediately recognize him as the predicted antichrist.

4

A Cowardly King
in Israel

A Cowardly King
in Israel

The epistles of John explicitly associate the antichrist with the liar and the deceiver of end times. Paul in II Thessalonians links the deceiver and the liar with the man of sin who performs miracles. Revelation 13 tells us that the deceiver and miracle-worker is the beast out of the earth. The beast out of the earth promotes the worship of the first beast. Now, does Scripture anywhere else describe such a relationship between two wicked end-time leaders? Daniel 11:36-39 is a definite possibility. Let us look at it.

Daniel has been predicting the wars that would occur between the Ptolemies (the kings of the south) and the Seleucidae (the kings of the north)—wars in which Israel would be overrun and ruined. Then, without a word of preparation or identification, Daniel introduces a person whom he merely calls "the king":

> "And the king shall do according to his will; and he shall exalt himself, and magnify himself above every god, and shall speak marvellous things against the God of gods, and shall prosper till the indignation be accomplished: for that that is determined shall be done" (Daniel 11:36).

Whoever the king is, he is so well-known that the word "the" is sufficient to identify him. *The* king implies the one whom every godly Jew expected to appear, much the same as *the* antichrist is the one whom every student of John and Paul expected to come. *The* king and *the* antichrist both appeared in Scripture suddenly and without any previous identification.

This similarity alone, however, would not be sufficient evidence for us to identify "the king" of Daniel 11:36 with the antichrist (the second beast of Revelation). In fact, the deification of the king sounds like the description of the first beast in Revelation 13:4-6:

> "And they worshipped the dragon which gave power unto the beast: and they worshipped the beast, saying, Who is like the beast? who is able to make war with him? And there was given unto him a mouth speaking great things and blasphemies; and power was given unto him to continue forty and two months. And he opened his mouth in blasphemy against God, to blaspheme his name, and his tabernacle, and them that dwell in heaven."

Before we jump to the conclusion that the king of Daniel 11:36 is the first beast of Revelation 13, however, let us remember that both beasts of Revelation 13 receive divine honors. The second beast exercises great power himself in Jerusalem and promotes the worship of his colleague in Rome. In order to decide which beast of Revelation is represented by the king of Daniel 11:36, we shall have to read a little further in the passage.

This blasphemous king pays no respect whatever to anyone:

> "Neither shall he regard the God of his fathers, nor the desire of women, nor regard any god: for he shall magnify himself above all" (Daniel 11:37).

This sounds like a Jewish expression—"the God of his fathers"; the God of Abraham, Isaac, and Jacob. Perhaps we have in this description a hint that the king is a Jew. If we had only this to go on, we could not press the point. But the next expression—"the desire of women"—also has a Jewish flavor. Many reliable commentators affirm that this phrase refers to the Messiah. Every woman in Judah desired to become the mother of the Messiah. He was the desire of nations (Haggai 2:7) and He was also the desire of Jewish women.

Besides these expressions, several other items lead Bible students to conclude that the antichrist will be a Jew. It is hard to believe that Israel would receive a Gentile Messiah. No Gentile could pose as Christ with any success.

A number of teachers believe that the antichrist will come from the tribe of Dan. Revelation 7:4-8 gives a list of the Jewish tribes whom God will seal for special service during the tribulation. The tribe of Dan is conspicuous by its absence. It is possible that the antichrist will come from Dan and will so dominate his tribe that only a handful of Danites will escape his clutches. A few Danites will be saved during the tribulation, for Dan reappears in the list of tribes that will function during the millennium (Ezekiel 48:1).

A further case for Dan comes from those who remind us that Dan was the first of the tribes to embrace idolatry in the past. Amos warns those who "swear by the sin of Samaria, and say, Thy god, O Dan, liveth" (Amos 8:14). If this has future implications, then in the tribulation Jews will be depending on a wicked descendant of Dan to secure the land by entering into an idolatrous alliance with the Roman prince.

The prophecy of dying Jacob describes Dan:

"Dan shall judge his people, as one of the tribes of Israel. Dan shall be a serpent by the way, an adder in the path, that biteth the horse heels, so that his rider shall fall backward" (Genesis 49:16, 17).

Genesis 3:15 speaks of Satan as a serpent. Will the tribe of Dan especially serve Satan's purpose to thwart the Messianic promises from being fulfilled? Bible students have toyed with this idea at least since the time of Irenaeus (A.D. 130-202), who first named Dan as the tribe of the antichrist.

The king of Daniel 11:36 renounces the God of Israel and the Messiah of Israel. This is equivalent to what the Apostle John says about the antichrist denying the Father and the Son. The antichrist relates in a special way to religious error.

After emphasizing in verses 36 and 37 of Daniel 11 that the king exalts himself and magnifies himself above every god, Daniel explains that the king does have a god whom he worships after all:

"But in his estate shall he honour the God of forces: and a god whom his fathers knew not shall he honour with gold, and silver, and with precious stones, and pleasant things" (Daniel 11:38).

We may infer from this verse that the king exalts himself by honoring the god of forces (or the god of fortresses).

The king not only receives divine honors for himself but promotes the honor of the god of fortresses. He honors a god very different from the God of Abraham, Isaac, and Jacob. The Jewish fathers would never recognize the god whom the king will serve. The king will pay dearly for his relationship to the god of fortresses—"gold, and silver, and with precious stones, and pleasant things."

But who or what is the god of fortresses? It must be the Roman prince who will preside over Europe's military strength during the last half of the tribulation. The first beast of Revelation 13 is both a political and a military leader. He is the dictator who will promise to defend Israel, provided Israel's false messiah will promote the worship of the dictator. The king of Daniel 11:36 is the second beast of Revelation 13, who will promote the worship of the first beast in order to get military protection against Arab or Russian aggressors.

Israel will be so eager to preserve the military alliance with the West she will be willing to do anything—including reintroducing idolatry to the land. The Israel of the tribulation period, through the negotiations of her false messiah, will bow to emperor worship.

By his relationship with the Roman dictator, the antichrist will cause the Romans to rule over Israel:

> "Thus shall he do in the most strong holds with a strange god, whom he shall acknowledge and increase with glory: and he shall cause them to rule over many, and shall divide the land for gain" (Daniel 11:39).

The forces of reorganized Rome will occupy Palestine and desecrate the temple area (Luke 21:24; Revelation 11:2). The antichrist will turn the land over to them.

The antichrist thinks of only one thing: How can I get more prominence, prestige, and power? He will take Israel into an unholy alliance with the military West in order to further his personal ambitions. He will promote emperor worship for selfish reasons. He will carve up the land of Palestine in order to please the people who can promote him. He will rob Israel of her natural resources in order to secure his own interests.

When we think of a king in Palestine who goes to idolatrous extremes in order to feather his own nest, we cannot help turning to Zechariah 11:15-17. Here just such a person comes to the fore:

> "And the Lord said unto me, Take unto thee yet the instruments of a foolish shepherd" (verse 15).

The shepherd is foolish in the sense that he is wicked, not in the sense that he is stupid. He carries the equipment of a shepherd, but he does not have a shepherd's heart. His gear makes people think he is a shepherd. He wears the outward insignia of a shepherd.

This shepherd will arise in the land of Palestine by divine providence:

> "For, lo, I will raise up a shepherd in the land, who

36

shall not visit those that are cut off, neither shall seek the young one, nor heal that that is broken, nor feed that that standeth still: but he shall eat the flesh of the fat, and tear their claws in pieces" (verse 16).

The kings of Israel were frequently called shepherds (Ezekiel 34:1-31). It was their duty to protect the people from aggressors. The shepherd-king of whom Zechariah speaks will not succeed in preventing invaders from penetrating the land and scattering the people. His alliances with the Western dictator cannot ultimately prevent the Russian invasion or check Arab hostilities against Israel (Daniel 11:40).

The attack upon Israel will cause another national dispersion of the Jews (Matthew 24:16-20). Many will be cut off from the home land. But the shepherd-king will make no attempt to comfort the exiles or to retrieve the wanderers. He will do nothing that a real shepherd would do in the time of crisis. He cares only about his own welfare. He bleeds the people; he lives at their expense. He is not satisfied until he has devoured every piece of all he can get.

When the danger is greatest, the foolish shepherd deserts the people:

> "Woe to the idol shepherd that leaveth the flock! the sword shall be upon his arm, and upon his right eye: his arm shall be clean dried up, and his right eye shall be utterly darkened" (Zechariah 11: 17).

During the invasions of Palestine, the antichrist will show his true colors. He will think first of his own safety and hide out somewhere until the northern and Arab invasions have subsided. Instead of remaining in the land to defend the Jewish people whom he represents, the false messiah will abandon the flock. By this cowardly act, many in Israel will realize that they have placed their trust in the wrong christ.

THE SHOWDOWN . . .

The Lord Jesus Christ referred to the incident of which Zechariah speaks. Christ contrasted Himself with the hireling shepherd. The hireling does his work only to get paid. He works for selfish reasons. He has no interest in the welfare of the sheep unless he gains something personally from it. When danger strikes, the hireling thinks first of his own neck:

> "But he that is an hireling, and not the shepherd, whose own the sheep are not, seeth the wolf coming, and leaveth the sheep, and fleeth: and the wolf catcheth them, and scattereth the sheep" (John 10:12).

If he hears an enemy approaching, he flees from the scene leaving the sheep at the mercy of the predator.

The hireling, of course, is the false messiah. The wolf represents the northern invader that will terrorize Israel soon after the middle of the tribulation period. The sheep are the Jews who will either flee the land or suffer injury or death in the invasions.

What a contrast the good shepherd is to the hireling shepherd. Jesus is the good shepherd. This means that He is the genuine, the real, and the true, as distinct from the counterfeit. The antichrist is the impostor. The genuine shepherd would rather lay down his life than leave the sheep to fall prey to the enemy:

> "I am the good shepherd: the good shepherd giveth his life for the sheep" (John 10:11)

This is exactly what the Lord Jesus Christ did. He sacrificed His life to save us.

At the end of the tribulation period Israel will at last enter into the benefits of the death of Christ. Israel will repudiate the false christ and receive the true Christ. When Israel's foes determine to annihilate the nation, Jesus will descend from Heaven and destroy the destroyers.

Although the antichrist will flee when Russia invades Palestine, he cannot escape the Lord Jesus when He returns to the earth. The Apostle Paul says that Christ will destroy the man of sin with the brightness of His coming (II Thessalonians 2:8). The Apostle John merely says that the beast (the Roman prince) and the false prophet (the Jewish antichrist) were taken (Revelation 19:20).

The context of Revelation 19 indicates that after Babylon perishes and the empire of the Roman prince crumbles, the armies of the Orient will face the armies of the Occident at Megiddo. Whether they fight each other for world supremacy we do not know. Suddenly Christ will come to slay the armies and cast the leaders into the lake of fire. The Roman prince and the Jewish deceiver acted together, and they will perish together.

One thousand years later, when Satan joins them, the Roman prince and the Jewish antichrist are still writhing in the lake of fire (Revelation 20:10). Thus the son of perdition at last meets his doom at the hand of the Son of man. The false christ will be unmasked by the true Christ. The wicked king of Palestine will have to give place to the King of kings and the Lord of lords.

What a day of victory and triumph that will be for the Lord of lords and the King of kings and those who descend from the Glory with Him. Will you be one of them or are you one of those who have scorned Him?

Today if you have not trusted the Saviour, you can. Tomorrow the age of grace may have ended, and then you cannot. Don't run the risk of having to meet Him as Judge. Trust Him today as your Saviour.

THE SHOWDOWN . . .

5

Early Preview
of the Antichrist

Early Preview
of the Antichrist

More and more we are pinpointing who the antichrist is and what he will do. In the preceding chapters we have recognized him as the man of sin, the son of perdition, the lawless one, the beast out of the earth, the false prophet, the false christ, the false messiah, the king who rules Palestine according to his own will, the idol shepherd of Zechariah 11, and the hireling shepherd of John 10. These are the principal references to and names of the antichrist.

Other end-time leaders also appear in Scripture. We have to pay strict attention so that we do not confuse them with the antichrist. The Roman prince is an end-time character whom we must carefully distinguish from the antichrist. The Roman prince does not appear in Scripture nearly as frequently as the antichrist does. The Roman prince is called the little horn in Daniel 7:8:

> "I considered the horns, and, behold, there came up among them another little horn, before whom there were three of the first horns plucked up by the roots: and, behold, in this horn were eyes like the eyes of man and a mouth speaking great things."

The little horn of Daniel 7 is the Roman prince of Daniel 9:26. Daniel says, in that verse, that the people of the prince that shall come will destroy the city of Jerusalem and the temple. The people who committed this act were the Romans, under General Titus in A.D. 70. The prince that shall come, then, originates from the people who destroyed Jerusalem—Roman people—hence, the Roman prince that shall come.

The little horn of Daniel 7, the prince, and the beast out of the sea are all one and the same. The beast out of the sea has "a mouth speaking great things and blasphemies" (Revelation 13:5). Daniel 7:8,20 are parallel verses. The book of Revelation refers to him repeatedly as simply "the beast"— that is, the first beast, the beast out of the sea.

The Roman prince and the Jewish antichrist are both blasphemers. Both of them attribute to themselves divine titles and divine privileges. They say things about themselves which are true only of God, and they attribute to God characteristics which are foreign and repulsive to the divine nature.

The Roman prince claims to be God almighty; he is the anti-God. The Jewish false prophet claims to be Christ; he is the anti-Christ. The devil or dragon is the spirit which enables the Roman prince and the Jewish prophet to rule the reorganized Roman empire; Satan is the anti-Spirit. And so, in these three persons you notice a caricature of the Trinity.

Another end-time leader will also dominate the scene of prophecy—the Russian desolator. As soon as you can distinguish the Roman dictator and the Jewish deceiver from the Russian desolator, you will be well on the way to mastering the prophetic Scriptures.

Isaiah calls the Russian desolator "the Assyrian" (Isaiah 10:5). Ezekiel refers to him as "Gog and Magog" (Ezekiel 38:2). "Chief prince" should probably be translated "Prince Rosh" (Ezekiel 38:3; 39:1). Daniel calls him "the king of the north" (Daniel 11:40). In chapter 8, Daniel speaks of him as "the king of fierce countenance." Joel identifies him as "the northern army" (Joel 2:20).

It is necessary to keep all of these identifications in mind in order to distinguish who the antichrist is. We need to know who he is by deciding who he isn't.

The antichrist is not the Assyrian, the king of the north, the little horn, the Roman prince, the beast out of the sea, and so forth. The antichrist is unique and distinct and not to be confused with other prophetic personages.

THE SHOWDOWN . . .

There are a few references to the antichrist which we have not yet mentioned. Some Bible teachers think the bloody and deceitful man in Psalm 5:6 is the antichrist. It may be that the fiery, flying serpent of Isaiah 14:29 has the antichrist in view. The prophecy was initially fulfilled in an apostate Jewish king, and perhaps it looks beyond him to the final apostate king of the Jews.

The false christs and false prophets of Matthew 24:4,5,24 will all culminate in the final false christ and false prophet. Conceivably, the antichrist will commission a team of representatives to promote his policies throughout the Middle East, just as Christ commissioned the Seventy and sent them out to represent Him. (Luke 10:1-17).

The abomination of desolation to which Daniel 12:11 and Matthew 24:15 refer is not the antichrist. It is a statue of the Roman prince which the Jewish antichrist will erect in the Jewish temple at Jerusalem.

John 5:43 probably refers to the antichrist. Jesus said:

> "I am come in my Father's name, and ye receive
> me not: if another shall come in his own name, him
> ye will receive."

Jesus came to the Israelitish fold by a legitimate entrance (John 10:1-5). He was the genuine Messiah who had all of His Messianic credentials in perfect order. His Father attested the genuineness of Christ's claim by an audible announcement from Heaven three times. The Jews of Jesus' day examined His credentials and concluded that He was a liar and a fraud.

When the false messiah appears with his fraudulent credentials, the national representatives of Israel will examine his claims and conclude that he is the long-anticipated Messiah. This is what makes Israel's future transgression so great. They abandoned the true for the false. They repudiated the Lord Jesus, but they will receive the antichrist.

Certain persons in Scripture are typical of the antichrist.

In these wicked persons we have a preview of the man of sin. Cain was such a person (Genesis 4:1-24). Cain manifested his wicked heart in religious activities, just as the antichrist is a religious figure. Sin was ready to pounce upon Cain and destroy him, just as the man of sin will be ruined in perdition. Cain murdered a brother as the result of a religious issue; this is the first religious war. Antichrist will carry out a religious war against his brethren the Jews. Cain was a liar; he denied a knowledge of his brother's fate. The antichrist is the final liar.

At first Cain was a fugitive, just as the antichrist will flee his home land. Then Cain founded a godless civilization in the East, just as antichrist will reorganize ancient Babylon. Cain was identified by a mark, just as the antichrist will have a mark to identify beast worshipers.

King Saul, as he ended his life a rebel from God, has characteristics in common with the antichrist (I Samuel 8:31). He was the choice of Israel at a time when the nation had rejected theocratic rule, just as the antichrist will be Israel's choice while they are still nationally rejecting the true Messiah. Israel thought Saul was the answer to their problems with aggressors, just as future Israel will depend upon the antichrist to defend Israel's borders.

Saul was a man of distinction; he was numbered among the prophets, he was a king, and he interfered in priestly functions. So, the antichrist is a prophet, priest, and king in Israel. Saul was a foolish shepherd, like the idol shepherd of Zechariah 11. Saul murdered those priests who identified with David, just as antichrist will murder the tribulation saints who trust David's greater son, Jesus Christ.

Saul's reign was followed by the reign of David, the man after God's own heart. After the brief reign of antichrist, King Jesus will sit upon David's throne forever. Saul became involved in spiritism and met with a sudden and ignominious death, just as the antichrist will be a demon-possessed man whom the Lord will slay suddenly.

The Herods of New Testament times are perhaps the best illustrations of the antichrist. Herod the Great was a king in

Israel (Matthew 2:1-23). He was a renegade Jew whom Mark Anthony confirmed in his kingdom in 37 B.C. Herod never ceased to support the emperor and promote his honor. He made Caesarea a center of Caesar worship in the land of the Jews.

Herod took an active interest in Jewish religious affairs; he even built the Jewish temple. He was a savage monster who massacred all Jews who opposed his policies. He determined to destroy the baby Jesus whom he considered a rival to the throne of Judea. In all of these respects he is a forerunner of the antichrist and a prototype of the antichrist's relationship to the Roman prince.

Herod Antipas perpetuated the Caesar cult. He depended upon the patronage of the emperor of Rome for his position in Palestine. He honored the emperor by building the city of Tiberias. He maintained his throne by cunning and subtle diplomacy. Jesus called him "that fox." Herod posed as a religious man who stood on his oath (Matthew 14:1-12). He lived in flagrant sin, defying the law of Moses. He was influenced by a wicked woman. He silenced the voice of God's special witness—John the Baptist.

In these matters Herod Antipas depicts the relationship the antichrist will sustain to the Roman prince and the Roman empire. He too is a trickster. He is the man of sin and the lawless one. He will consort with the harlot woman of Revelation 17 during the first half of the tribulation. He will murder God's witnesses.

Herod Agrippa I has all of the earmarks of the antichrist (Acts 12:1-4, 20-23). Another renegade Jew, he was king in Israel while Caesar reigned in Rome. He killed the Lord's witness, James, with the sword and afflicted the Jewish saints. He was too religious to murder the Apostle Peter during the days of unleavened bread. He imposed a food boycott on Tyre and Sidon. He was an eloquent orator. He accepted divine worship while recognizing the deity of Claudius Caesar. He was smitten suddenly by a divine judgment.

Simon Magus is a dead ringer for the antichrist (Acts 8:5-

24). He professed to be a Christian but turned out to be an apostate. He was a renegade Jew who dabbled in the occult. He deified himself in the eyes of his followers. He magnetized everyone—from the least to the greatest. He aspired to perform miracles and so asked for the gift of the Spirit. His chief interest was commerce; he thought he could buy and sell religious powers. He was the quintessence of wickedness, and his heart was a gall of bitterness. Peter said he would perish; he was destined for perdition.

Church history affords us many an illustration of the role antichrist will play. The Emperor Charlemagne and Pope Leo III are predecessors of the Roman prince and the antichrist—one political and the other religious. Henry VIII and Cardinal Wolsey are a similar combination. Wherever you have a union of church and state, you have a potential political dictator and a religious deceiver who strive for uncontested supremacy. This combination has always resulted in the martyrdom of true believers, for they will never bow to the unholy marriage of church and state.

It is no wonder that the Reformers almost unanimously identified the antichrist with the pope. The Reformers correctly understood that the antichrist would be predominately a religious figure, an apostate, a seducer, and a destroyer of the truth of God. It is doubtful, however, that any present or future pope can be the antichrist—unless, of course, somehow the college of cardinals elects a Jew to the papal office.

When the antichrist finally makes his entry upon the stage of history, he will be, surely, an apostate Jew who will enjoy the support of the final Roman Caesar. He will employ the power of the state to execute those who refuse to become beast worshipers. Once more the blood of the martyrs will flow (Revelation 6:9-11; 17:6; 18:24).

At the beginning of the tribulation period the antichrist will succeed in getting an official and formal treaty of peace between Israel and her Arab neighbors (Isaiah 18:15; Daniel 9:27). The document will define Israel's exact borders. Israel will withdraw to these recognized territories. The Arabs will concede to Israel's right to exist in these domains. The Arabs will probably acknowledge Israel's statehood.

Israel will be willing to withdraw from the occupied territories because the treaty will guarantee Israel the protection of a superpower in the event that anyone (either the Russians or the Arabs) encroaches upon Israeli soil. Israel will lean the full weight of her confidence upon the promises of the antichrist, who will negotiate this treaty. For several months peace will prevail in the Mid East (Revelation 6:1-4). Israel will relax. The Mosaic ritual will begin in the rebuilt Jewish temple.

Then in the middle of the tribulation the Roman prince will come to dictatorial power. He will instruct the Jews to place a statue of himself in the holy of holies. He will make this the condition by which Israel receives continued military support from the superpowers in the West. He will deify Israel's national representative—the Jewish antichrist.

Israel has longed for peace for such a long time that she will be willing to do anything to preserve it once it comes. Therefore, the Jews will permit the antichrist to erect the image of the Roman dictator in the temple. Israel as a whole will engage in idolatrous worship. Those godly Jews who refuse to participate in emperor worship will face the martyr's pyre. The nation will learn too late that it has trusted a deceiver and a liar.

Prophecy demonstrates how perilous it is to trust the wrong person. It is dangerous to misplace your hopes. Those who rest their full weight upon the promises of God and upon the Lord Jesus Christ will never be disappointed (I Peter 2:6). He will prove all that He claims to be. If you have put your confidence in politicians, priests, preachers, or human potential, transfer that confidence to the only One who is worthy of it. Jesus Christ the Lord is your only hope of salvation and safety.

6

Confusion Over End-Time Leaders

Confusion Over
End-Time Leaders

Before moving on to the dramatic climax of the end times—the Battle of Armageddon—let us pause to consider the principal actors that will figure in prophecy. It is necessary for us to clear the air of the confusion that surrounds these characters in the minds of students of prophecy. To do so, we shall have to examine briefly the contradicting views which have been presented about the end-time personnel.

From the simple induction method of study of the Scriptures which we have been pursuing, we have arrived at certain conclusions concerning the identity of the antichrist and other important prophetic personages mentioned in Scripture. We have recognized the antichrist as the man of sin, the son of perdition, the lawless one, the beast out of the earth, the second beast, the false prophet, the false christ, the false messiah, the king who rules Palestine according to his own will, the idol shepherd, and the hireling shepherd.

The Western dictator, on the other hand, is the Roman prince of Daniel 9:26, the little horn of Daniel 7:8, the beast out of the sea, the first beast (sometimes called the marine beast), and the one whom John the apostle simply calls "the beast." Of all the end-time characters, Scripture says the least about this one.

The Russian desolator is known also as the Assyrian, Gog and Magog, the king of the north, the king of fierce countenance, and the northern army. The Scripture says the most about this character.

As we have examined the Scriptures together, these end-time personages seem relatively clear, do they not? But when we read the writings of prophetic commentators—all able, Christ-honoring authors—we find that confusion reigns on the subject of the antichrist. No less than fifty Biblical titles have been given to the antichrist, often confusing him with other end-time personnel.

Rather than adding to the confusion, the following summary is intended to help clarify the problem by noting the main views and the groups of Bible teachers which hold them. A knowledge of the differences will help the inquisitive reader toward arriving at his own conclusions based upon careful study of the passages involved.

A comparison of the prophetic writers will show that essentially three interpretations prevail.

1. According to the first interpretation, the little horn of Daniel 7, the little horn of Daniel 8, the Roman prince of Daniel 9:26, the king of Daniel 11:36, the man of sin of II Thessalonians 2:3, and the beast out of the sea in Revelation 13:1-10 are all identical with the antichrist of I John 2:18 and II John 7.

Writers for this school of thought include John F. Walvoord, J. Dwight Pentecost, Charles Ryrie, and generally speaking, all of the students and public who are influenced by these widely read interpreters. The faculty of Dallas Theological Seminary did not originate this interpretation, but they do perpetuate it. For convenience we shall call this the Dallas school of thought.

The Dallas interpreters tend to identify the rider on the white horse in Revelation 6:4 with the antichrist. This view teaches that Daniel 11:41-45 describes the conquests and ultimate defeat of the antichrist. The view distinguishes the antichrist from Gog and Magog, the king of the north, and the Assyrian. Except for a few interpreters like Clarence Larkin, Lehman Strauss, and Ford Ottman, this school believes that the antichrist is a Gentile politician and a military strategist.

With a few minor differences the following writers hold substantially the Dallas view: Philip R. Newell, William

Newell, Erich Sauer, Alva J. McClain, Robert D. Culver, Walter K. Price, Leon Wood, Clarence Larkin, William Pettingil, Louis Talbot, Gary Cohen, and Merrill Unger.

2. The second school of interpreters contradicts the Dallas view at nearly every point. This view is characteristically William Kelly's interpretation and was popularized by Arno C. Gaebelein (long-time editor of *Our Hope* magazine). For convenience we shall designate it as the Kelly-Gaebelein school of interpretation.

The Kelly-Gaebelein view states that the title "antichrist" does not belong on the little horn of Daniel 7, the little horn of Daniel 8, the Roman prince of Daniel 9:26, or the beast out of the sea. This school insists that the antichrist is the king of Daniel 11:36, the man of sin of II Thessalonians 2:3, the beast out of the earth of Revelation 13:11-18, and the false prophet of Revelation 19:20. This view teaches that the antichrist and the false prophet are one and the same person. It holds that the antichrist is a Jew and a religious apostate rather than a Gentile politician.

The Kelly-Gaebelein school agrees with the Dallas view in the following particulars: (1) The king of Daniel 11:36 and the man of sin in II Thessalonians 2:3 should have the title "antichrist" applied to them; (2) The Assyrian, the king of the north, and Gog and Magog are not the antichrist.

These two schools of prophetic interpretation disagree over the identification of Daniel 11:41-45. The Kelly-Gaebelein view teaches that these verses describe the conquests and defeat of the king of the north, who marches his armies to North Africa and comes to an inglorious end when he attempts to attack Israel en route from North Africa to his home base. The Dallas view agrees that these verses describe the conquests and defeat of the Roman prince, whom the Dallas school equates with the antichrist.

The Kelly-Gaebelein school says that the little horn of

Daniel 8 typifies the king of the north, not the antichrist and not the Roman prince. The Dallas school thinks that this little horn prefigures the Roman prince. The Kelly-Gaebelein school fails to see in Antiochus Epiphanes a type of the antichrist; rather, he is a type of the coming king of the north who is also called the Assyrian and Prince Rosh, or the Russian desolator. The Dallas school explains that Antiochus Epiphanes is a type of the Roman prince, whom Dallas equates with the antichrist.

Writers for the Kelly-Gaebelein school of thought include E. Schuyler English, Charles Feinberg, Arno C. Gaebelein, James M. Gray, L. Sale-Harrison, F.W. Grant, Harry Ironside, William Kelly, E. W. Rogers, Walter Scott, James Scott, and Frederick Tatford. The older Plymouth Brethren writers all follow essentially the Kelly-Gaebelein view.

3. A third school of interpreters equates virtually all of the titles of end-time leaders with the antichrist. They believe that even Gog and Magog, the king of the north, and the Assyrian are designations for the antichrist. These writers include G. H. Lang, A. W. Pink, and Geoffrey King. Philip Newell holds mainly the Dallas view, except that he makes the king of the north the antichrist. He thinks that the willful king of Daniel 11:36 is also the king of the north, and this is at variance with the Dallas view.

A number of other writers are a bit more difficult to classify. Hal Lindsey and S. F. Logsdon, for instance, follow substantially the Dallas view but differ with it in that they interpret Daniel 11:41-45 as the conquests and defeat of the king of the north rather than of the Roman prince. W. E. Blackstone belongs to the Kelly-Gaebelein school, except that he sees the king of Babylon as a type of the false prophet, whereas the Kelly-Gaebelein school interprets the king of Babylon to be a type of the Roman prince. F. C. Jennings follows the Kelly-Gaebelein view, except that Jennings believes that the Assyrian is not a counterpart of Prince Rosh.

THE SHOWDOWN . . .

C. I. Scofield follows the Kelly-Gaebelein view, for Scofield equates the antichrist with the false prophet. Scofield writes in his note in the 1917 edition of the Scofield Reference Bible, pages 1342-1343:

> The "many antichrists" precede and prepare the way for the Antichrist, who is "the Beast out of the earth" of Rev. 13:11-17, and the "false prophet" of Rev. 16:13; 19:20; 20:10. He is the last ecclesiastical head, as the Beast of Rev. 13:1-8 is the last civil head.

But Scofield teaches also that the man of sin is the Roman prince, and the Kelly-Gaebelein school refutes this. Scofield taught that the little horn of Daniel 8 is a type of the antichrist, whereas the Kelly-Gaebelein view says that the little horn of Daniel 8 is a type of the king of the north.

E. W. Rogers follows the Kelly-Gaebelein school, except that Rogers thinks the man of sin is the Roman prince. Frederick Tatford also follows the Gaebelein school, and yet at one point he strays away from it by calling the man of sin the Roman prince. In his commentary on Daniel, however, Tatford clearly teaches that the man of sin is the Jewish king and not the Roman prince.

J. Allen Blair calls the little horn of Daniel 7, the little horn of Daniel 8, and the willful king of Daniel 11:36-39 the antichrist. He calls the man of sin the antichrist. Then he distinguishes the antichrist from the Roman beast. Some of the same inconsistencies appear in the comments of Dr. M. R. DeHaan and of Oliver Green; they couldn't make up their mind which school of interpretation to follow.

Clarence Mason seems to favor the Kelly-Gaebelein school, for he teaches that the willful king of Daniel 11:36 is the Jewish king in Palestine rather than the Roman prince. Dr. Mason, however, does not follow through with the Kelly-Gaebelein view of Daniel 11:41-45. He thinks that the Jewish king rather than the king of the north makes the conquests in North Africa and suffers defeat.

To compound the confusion thoroughly, Hal Lindsey concludes in his 1973 book, *There's a New World Coming,* that there are two antichrists. Clarence Mason also has suggested that perhaps both of the beasts in Revelation 13 deserve the title "antichrist." This, of course, will solve nothing; for on this basis, no one will be able to distinguish all of the titles that belong to the first beast (the Roman prince) and all of the titles that belong to the second beast (the false prophet).

The Dallas school of interpreters sees in Scripture a final trinity of evil according to the following identifications:

The Anti-God	=	The dragon, devil, and Satan
The Anti-Christ	=	The beast out of the sea, the Roman prince
The Anti-Spirit	=	The beast out of the earth, the false prophet

The Kelly-Gaebelein school of interpreters also sees in Scripture a final trinity of evil, but these interpreters propose the following identifications:

The Anti-God	=	The beast out of the sea, the Roman prince
The Anti-Christ	=	The beast out of the earth, the false prophet
The Anti-Spirit	=	The dragon, devil, and Satan

In the last analysis every student of prophetic Scriptures will have to resolve these many differences for himself. It is doubtful that anyone can become thoroughly comfortable with Biblical prophecy until he has untangled the three distinct end-time personages and has learned the various Biblical titles that apply to each of these personages. A mastery of prophecy demands that the student distinguish the Roman prince with his various aliases from the Jewish antichrist with his aliases and from the Russian destroyer with his aliases.

THE SHOWDOWN . . .

Our inductive approach to Bible study has led us straight to the Kelly-Gaebelein interpretation of end-time actors. Many illustrious Bible teachers have championed this view for well over 100 years. In recent times it has fallen into obscurity for lack of anyone to keep it before the Christian reader. Gradually the Dallas view has come to the front and has supplanted the older view. Nevertheless, the Kelly-Gaebelein view is self-consistent and clarifies prophetic distinctions satisfactorily.

Recently a man who is just approaching retirement age spoke to me. He has given his whole adult life to studying and teaching prophecy. He has written considerably on this subject. He has served in Bible institutes and Bible colleges. During all of this time the man has presented the Dallas interpretation of end-time events and personages. For some reason he decided to set aside everything and with only his Bible work through the field of Biblical prophecy again. He told me that this has resulted in conclusions very similar to my own (that is, to the Kelly-Gaebelein view).

Someone else might arrive at quite a different conclusion from a similar exercise, but each one will have to work through the problem for himself. A firm grasp of the prophetic Word rests in large part upon precision in the identification of end-time characters. The characters shape the prophetic events, and so, to confuse the characters makes chaos of the prophetic events.

7

The Arab Contribution to Armageddon

The Arab Contribution
to Armageddon

Armageddon. That name has struck fear into the human heart for nineteen centuries. It is synonymous with the war to end all wars. It contemplates a military confrontation on a worldwide scale. To all people — Christian and non-Christian — Armageddon stands for the final holocaust of history and the doom of civilization as we know it. Armageddon is a picture of nations rushing to their doom. It is a terrifying concept, isn't it?

Armageddon is more than a universal symbol to represent the most destructive war in human history. It is a literal event which Bible prophecy anticipates and describes in considerable detail. Armageddon is not only real but near. Right now you can see the nations jockeying for the positions they will hold when Armageddon sweeps them into oblivion. *How soon will the nations plunge into World War III? Will we live to see it? Will anyone survive it?*

Before we can answer these questions intelligently, we need to set the stage of prophecy. We need a proper background in order to evaluate the significance of Armageddon's earth-shaking effects.

The very first event scheduled on the prophetic calendar is the removal of every living believer. The Lord Jesus Christ will come into the vicinity of our earth and transport believers to Heaven bodily (I Thessalonians 4:16,17). Instead of dying, we believers shall end our days on earth in the same manner as Elijah and Enoch. God translated Enoch to Heaven just before the universal flood broke upon the earth, and the Lord will catch away living believers just before the universal judgments of the tribulation period strike the earth. We usually refer to this removal of the true church as the rapture.

The rapture of the church is the first sign which will indicate to the people of earth that the coming of Jesus Christ to earth to set up His kingdom is near. The rapture of the church is the signal for the beginning of a seven-year period in which God works to overthrow all who oppose His plans. It will be a time of unprecedented trouble for Israel and for the Gentile nations (Daniel 12:1). Disasters unparalleled in the history of the world will depopulate and deface the planet. This seven-year period is called the tribulation.

In the earliest hours of the tribulation period Israel will ratify a treaty with a ten-nation federation in the Mediterranean world (Daniel 9:27). This event takes for granted that Israel at that time will be a sovereign state among the other nations of the world. It also takes for granted that ten Mediterranean countries will unite economically and militarily. A United States of Europe will come into existence, consisting of ten cooperating nations (Daniel 7:24). The newly organized federation will guarantee military protection to Israel. The treaty promises to defend Israel from an attack by hostile armies.

The present state of affairs in Europe and the Middle East tends to confirm the Biblical prophecies, don't you agree? Israel became a nation in 1948. The United States of Europe is already a possibility. It got underway in 1948, when Belgium, Holland, and Luxembourg (Benelux) entered economic agreements. Later, Germany, France, and Italy cooperated. In January of 1973 Great Britain, Ireland, and Denmark joined the growing community. When the organization is complete, it will consist of ten nations (Revelation 17:12).

It is the trend of the West to protect Israel, as the Eisenhower Doctrine states. The West has sold Israel sophisticated weapons. No formal military agreement yet exists. Israel has only a gentleman's agreement with the United States. The U.S. has made it amply clear that it will maintain the balance of power in the Middle East by supplying defensive equipment to Israel.

Israel's foes are numerous. Arab kingdoms surround Israel, each breathing out threatenings and slaughter. Fomenting Arab hatred, Russia has made her presence increasingly felt in the Middle East, although in the last several months Russian influence has been waning. Still, for all practical purposes the Mediterranean today is a Russian lake. The old rabbis used to say that when Russia penetrates the Dardanelles, the Jewish people should expect the Messiah to come.

The military alliance between Israel and the coming United States of Europe will convince Israel she has nothing to fear from her enemies. She will rest confidently upon the assurances which the West guarantees (Isaiah 28:15-18). Israeli leaders will relax, thinking that peace and safety have at last come to secure Israel's borders (Ezekiel 38:8,11,14).

But when they say peace and safety, sudden destruction will come upon them (I Thessalonians 5:3). The era of peace is all too brief. It is only a lull before the storm breaks. Israel's relationship with the surrounding nations and with her Western allies leads to Armageddon. Palestine is the vortex which will draw all nations to destruction. One by one they will venture into Emmanuel's land and meet their doom.

The battle of Armageddon is a much more complicated event than many of us may realize. Revelation 16:16 is the only place in Scripture where the word "Armageddon" occurs. Verse 14 mentions "the battle of that great day of God Almighty." You put the two verses together, and you have "the battle of Armageddon"—that is, the battle which will take place at Megiddo. In the last fifty years thousands of books on prophecy have flooded the Christian market, and one author contradicts another in his explanation of the battle of Armageddon. As with many topics of prophecy, confusion reigns on the subject of Armageddon.

L. Sale-Harrison thinks that Armageddon is a conflict between the United States of Europe and Russia. Harry

Ironside teaches that Armageddon is a conflict between the United States of Europe and the powers of Asia. William Pettingill says Armageddon is a conflict between all nations and God. Alva J. McClain sees it as a conflict between four great world powers. Milton Lindberg interprets it to be a conflict between the United States of Europe, Russia, and Asia. W. W. Fereday explains that Russia is not involved in Armageddon. Harry Rimmer writes that Russia is the only aggressor at Armageddon. The only apparent point of agreement in all of these views is that Armageddon is a conflict.

When good and godly men differ on points of interpretation, it is wise for us to look for some way to harmonize the seeming contradictions. Is it possible that most of the interpretations above are correct? Can they be harmonized? If so, how? The solution lies in a correct understanding of the Greek word *polemos,* translated "battle" in Revelation 16:14. The word *polemos* does not refer to a single, isolated battle but to a war—a long military campaign. We would be more precise in our description if we learned to speak of the battle as the campaign of Armageddon.

The campaign of Armageddon is much more than a mere six-day war. It will rage over most of the last three years and six months of the tribulation period. The Valley of Megiddo is not the only place which will be involved in this long military campaign. The Valley of Jehoshaphat (Joel 3:2) and the region of Edom (Isaiah 63:1-3) are also scenes of the war. In fact, the whole of Palestine will be drenched in blood as military movements carry armies over the length and breadth of the land (Revelation 14:20).

During the final three and one-half years of the tribulation no less than four campaigns will reduce Palestine to rubble. The war of Armageddon will commence when Arab North Africa unites to assault Israel. Immediately afterward, Russia and all of her satellites will invade Israel from the north. In due time the Western allies will move their armies into Israel. Finally the Asiatic powers will back the

THE SHOWDOWN ...

Western powers into the Valley of Megiddo.

Now do you understand how so many discrepancies among the Bible teachers can be harmonized? As a long, three and one-half year campaign, Armageddon can include Russia, Egypt, the United States of Europe, and the Oriental armies. It remains to be seen just which great confederation of nations fight which other great confederation of nations. Does Russia fight the United States of Europe or does she fight the Asiatic powers, or whom? Armageddon, as a war involving a series of assaults upon the Middle East, takes all of these matters into account.

Let's begin at the beginning. At a time when Israel is depending upon military protection from the West and is therefore dwelling in fancied safety (Amos 6:1), the combined forces of North Africa will launch an unprovoked attack upon Israel from the south. Daniel 11:40a supplies us with this information. "And at the time of the end [the tribulation period] shall the king of the south [Egypt—in North Africa—and her confederates] push at him [the Jewish antichrist who will convince apostate Jews he is the Messiah]."

We may be reasonably certain that although the king of the south was certainly Egypt during the period before Christ's first coming and will be Egypt in the future, the king of the south in the time of the end will include more nations than just Egypt. Daniel 11:42 specifically names Egypt, but verse 43 associates Egypt with Libya and Ethiopia.

In all likelihood, Dr. Clarence Mason is correct when he argues that the king of the south includes the whole interior of Africa. He points out that ancient maps call the interior of Africa "Libya." Since this is almost exclusively Arab territory—in the sense of being dominated by the religion of Islam—perhaps it is not too much to conclude that the king of the south will include most of the Arab nations in the Middle East as well as in Africa. Ishmael, in the person of his descendants, will resolve to destroy Jacob, in the person of his descendants.

We have not only the assurances of prophecy to corroborate the actuality of this attack, but we also have four
recent attempts on the part of the Arabs to destroy Israel—
attempts in 1948, 1955, 1967, and 1973. Each time Israel
successfully repelled the aggressor. The Arabs still smart
from the humiliation of failure. They will never be satisfied
until they have settled the score.

After the 1967 assault Egypt counted on Russian technology to equip her for retaliation. We all expected Egypt to
launch the Russian missiles against Israel and recapture
the Sinai desert. Then unexpectedly in 1972 Egypt ordered
Russia out. Since then the Arab world is not so dependent
upon Russia. They have gained a more independent status
by using the oil embargo as a lever to pry away Western
support for Israel.

Will the Russian presence in the Mid East eventually
decline? That remains to be seen; but when the Arab
countries of North Africa try to destroy Israel in a final
attempt to possess all of Palestine with its vast natural
resources, Russia will no longer keep at bay. Russia cannot
permit the Arabs to control such a strategic place; it would
thwart Russia's own ambition to control the area. Then too,
Russia knows that any Arab invasion into Israel from the
south would draw the United States into the conflict.
Russia wishes to avoid a confrontation with the United
States—at least for the moment.

Consequently, when North Africa (perhaps most of the
Arab world) attacks Israel, Russia will intervene in order to
wrench oil out of Arab control and to keep the U.S. and
Europe from taking drastic action.

When students of Bible prophecy talked one generation
ago about Egypt invading Israel, they left themselves wide
open to ridicule. Unbelievers scoffed because neither Israel
nor Egypt existed as an independent nation. Nothing
indicated that circumstances would or could change. A
British mandate controlled Palestine, and Egypt was a
British protectorate.

If you had predicted in 1918 that the Balfour Declaration

would carve out of Palestine a place for Jews to begin a new nation or that a Nasser would arise and carry Egypt to lofty heights of power and prominence, your friends would have questioned your sanity. Egypt was hardly more than a sand dune, a place that attracted only archaeologists.

We have all lived to see a remarkable change in the Middle East—a change that God's Word anticipated all along. If we can learn anything from the rise of Israel and Egypt it is that God's Word is absolutely reliable. We can rest our full weight upon all of its pronouncements— prophetic and otherwise. When you stand on what God has said, you will probably be laughed at, but in the long run God will vindicate His Word and also the Christian who believes His Word.

A passionate hatred for another race will drive Egypt to attack Israel and in the process start World War III. This fact holds a lesson for all of us. We never know what a chain reaction of terrible events we might start by some rash deed motivated by an unsympathetic attitude toward someone different from us. Egypt may strike us as a nonentity, but her action will plunge the world into the last terrible conflict. As the Bible says, our tongue might seem like a little member, but it can set the whole world ablaze (James 3:5,6). Every action counts for good or ill. Let's start a chain reaction of good will and kind deeds.

8
Russia's Role
in Armageddon

Russia's Role
in Armageddon

An unprovoked attack upon Israel is the spark that ignites the war of Armageddon. Russian retaliation is swift, for the Russians immediately take military measures to deal with Arab arrogance.

Daniel 11:40-43 describes Russia's maneuvers:

> "And at the time of the end shall the king of the south push at him: and the king of the north shall come against him like a whirlwind, with chariots, and with horsemen, and with many ships; and he shall enter into the countries, and shall overflow and pass over.

> "He shall enter also into the glorious land, and many countries shall be overthrown: but these shall escape out of his hand, even Edom, and Moab, and the chief of the children of Ammon.

> "He shall stretch forth his hand also upon the countries: and the land of Egypt shall not escape.

> "But he shall have power over the treasures of gold and of silver, and over all the precious things of Egypt: and the Libyans and the Ethiopians shall be at his steps."

And Daniel 11:44,45 predicts Russia's ultimate defeat:

> "But tidings out of the east and out of the north shall trouble him: therefore he shall go forth with

great fury to destroy, and utterly to make away many.

"And he shall plant the tabernacles of his palace between the seas in the glorious holy mountain; yet he shall come to his end, and none shall help him."

The Russian invasion of Israel is the result of a variety of factors. Russia wants the natural resources of the Middle East for herself (Ezekiel 38:12); she cannot afford to let the Arabs control it. The Arab attack upon Israel forces Russia to invade. In the middle of the tribulation, Satan is cast out of his abode in the airways and confined to earth. In his fury he decides to annihilate Israel (Revelation 12:7-13). He will seek someone to do the work of liquidation. Russia is notoriously anti-Semitic, and so Satan will inspire the Russian armies to descend upon Palestine (Revelation 9:1-21)

There is still another factor to be considered. In the middle of the tribulation period a Gentile dictator will arise in Europe who will dominate world politics. The ten-nation federation will eventually give him absolute authority (Revelation 17:12,13). When he comes to power, he will notify Israel that the United States of Europe will not honor its military treaty with Israel unless the Jews permit their false prophet to erect a statue of the Gentile dictator in the rebuilt Temple (Daniel 9:27).

The Jews will be so eager to keep the alliance intact, they will consent to this arrangement (Matthew 24:15). Jews will worship the Gentile dictator by bowing to his image. Idolatry will once again infect the land of Israel (Revelation 13:14,15). The Jewish false prophet (the antichrist) will promote the worship of the Gentile dictator (Revelation 13:12). Together, these two end-time personalities will control politics and religion, military power and commercial enterprise.

When Israel consents to practice idolatry in order to get continued military aid from Western Europe, God will initiate proceedings against her. He will punish Israel by sending the Russian destroyer into her land (Isaiah 10:5,6). The erection of the idol in the Temple is the signal for the start of the Russian invasion (Matthew 24:15-21).

You can understand that many events will occur almost simultaneously or at least in trip-hammer sequence to bring Russia into the land of Israel. Russia will have her own intentions: (1) to prevent Egypt from controlling the Middle East; (2) to use Egypt's attack upon Israel as an occasion to occupy the Middle East and seize the natural resources for herself.

Satan has his own designs to annihilate Israel, and so he uses Russia's natural hatred and covetousness as a means of inspiring the invasion.

God has His plans to work out too. He will employ Russia to punish Israel for entering into a diabolical deal that involves idolatry. All of these factors will converge in the middle of the tribulation, and Russia will invade Israel.

The prophet Ezekiel graphically describes this in Ezekiel 38. Armies will descend upon Israel from the uttermost parts of the north—north of Israel (verse 15). The Bible describes an invasion by Gog of the land of Magog (verse 2). Gog is the leader; Magog is the people or the land. Prince Rosh is the instigator of the invasion. His territories are Meshech and Tubal. Meshech represents European Russia; Tubal represents Asiatic Russia. Meshech is the ancient word for Moscow. Tubal is the ancient word for Tobolski. Tobolski is the place where Commander Gary Powers was shot down in the U-2 incident during Khrushchev's term in the Kremlin.

A great company of nations will accompany Russia in her assault upon Israel (verse 15). Persia, Ethiopia, Libya, Gomer, and Togarmah will participate (verses 5,6). Ancient Persia is modern Iran. Gomer is probably Germany and other Teutonic people. Togarmah is eastern Turkey. Ethiopia and Libya are North African nations, and later on we shall learn how they come into the orbit of Russia's influence. Suffice it to say, the northern confederacy against Israel is enormous. John puts the number of horsemen at two hundred million (Revelation 9:16).

En route to Israel, the armies of Russia and her satellites will work a terrible destruction upon those parts of the Arab world which lie north of Israel. Isaiah describes the Russian invasion under the figure of the king of Assyria (Isaiah 8:7). Gog and the ancient king of Assyria, Sennacherib, have much in common. The Assyrian was an early predecessor of Russia with her allies. God plans to use the future Assyrians (Russia) to punish Israel for her hypocrisy (Isaiah 10:5,6). In the process of the invasion the future Assyrian will destroy many cities en route to Israel. Damascus will fall; this indicates the defeat of Syria (Isaiah 17:1-14). Tyre will capitulate; this suggests the defeat of Lebanon (Isaiah 23:1-18). The fortifications of Moab will surrender; this means the defeat of Jordan (Isaiah 15:1—16:14).

All of the defeated armies of Syria, Lebanon, and Jordan will combine with the Russian troops to swell the ever-increasing army. Persia will be included; this means that Iran is involved with Russia in the invasion (Ezekiel 38:5). We cannot be certain whether Iran will be a participating party from the beginning or whether Russia will defeat Iran and add the conquered army to the Russian ranks.

With the combined forces of Germany (and perhaps the Scandinavian countries), Turkey, Iraq, Iran, Syria, Lebanon, and Jordan, Russia will penetrate the borders of Israel. The whole land will lie under the weight of the invasion. In the path of the invasion the land is green with vegetation; in the wake of the army the land is desolate and ruined (Joel 2:1-3).

The invaders take city after city. Then for some strange reason the army tarries at Nob (Isaiah 10:32). This unexpected, temporary halt will give Jews time to escape to the remote places of Jordan, where they will find safety (Isaiah 16:1-4). The Lord prevents Russia from entering into these recesses (Daniel 11:41). Then, even more strangely, the Russian armies bypass the city of Jerusalem

(Zechariah 9:8). Remember, the Russians have come to drive the forces of North Africa out of Israel. In their eagerness to deal with Egypt, the armies of the north give Jerusalem a reprieve.

Steadily they advance southward. The armies do not stop until they have occupied Egypt, Ethiopia, and Libya (Daniel 11:42,43). The peninsula of Arabia also falls to the Russian conqueror (Isaiah 23:13-17). Without a doubt the defeated armies of Egypt, Libya, Ethiopia, and Arabia are added to the Russian forces.

In the southward push through Israel to North Africa, Russia succeeds in devastating the whole Middle East (Revelation 8:7-13), wiping out all opposition and increasing the size of its own army with the armies of defeated nations. God thus will use Russia to punish Israel for idolatry. God will use Russia to destroy the religion of Islam and the Arab coalition.

The whole Middle East will reel under the staggering blow of the Russian invasion. Meanwhile, it appears that the United States of Europe is slow to fulfill its treaty obligations with Israel. You can imagine the United Nations registering a series of protests against the daring Russian assault (Ezekiel 38:13). There is some confusion in the minds of Western politicians about Russia's real intent. Does Russia intend only to put the Arabs in their place, or is Russia only using the Arab invasion as an excuse to advance her own interests in the Middle East, gain a foothold, and stay?

While Israel's Western allies are deciding upon a course of action, Russia (with the bulk of her forces in Egypt) hears rumors from the northeast that force her hand: "But tidings out of the east and out of the north shall trouble him . . ." (Daniel 11:44a). They may learn that the Western allies of Israel have landed at Haifa. Or, the rumor may be some hint that the Asiatic forces are beginning to advance from beyond the Euphrates River. Perhaps the rumors include news of both of these events. At any rate, Russia cannot afford to get cut off from her home base by an invading army from the West and another one from the East. The Russians may realize that their defeat is certain.

With these problems confronting Russia in Egypt, the Russians with their allies decide to march northward into Israel and make a full end of Israel even if they cannot make it back to the Russian border (Daniel 11:44b). Doubtlessly the devil inspires Russia's determination to wipe Israel from the map. The armies, therefore, swing northward with Jerusalem in their sights. The colossal army makes its headquarters somewhere in the wilderness of Jordan or Judea—between the Mediterranean Sea and the Dead Sea (Daniel 11:45).

At an appropriate moment the armies move against Jerusalem from the south. They get no farther than the mountains of Judea when God comes to the defense of Jerusalem by causing an earthquake to swallow up vast numbers of the aggressor (Ezekiel 38:19). Meteorological phenomena will contribute to the supernatural destruction of the Russian army (verse 22). In their confusion the soldiers will commence to fight each other (verse 21). Some of the infantry will wander out into the area of the Dead Sea and perish in the desert sands (Joel 2:20). Jerusalem will never capitulate to the Communistic hordes from the north. God will intervene. He will destroy the destroyer. Only a fraction of the army will survive this divine judgment, and they will limp their way back to Siberia (Ezekiel 39:2)

We have a preview of the whole event in the experience of Sennacherib, king of Assyria (Isaiah 36:1—37:38). He too invaded Israel and drove his army to Egypt. Returning from Egypt, he decided to take Jerusalem, where Hezekiah and the Jews had barricaded themselves. Sennacherib demanded an unconditional surrender. Hezekiah waited and prayed for a divine deliverance. In the morning 185,000 Assyrians lay dead. God had sent an angel to smite the arrogant foe. Sennacherib and a few of his men returned to Assyria, defeated and disgraced.

During the Russian invasion, you may wonder where the false Jewish Messiah has stationed himself. In the months preceding the invasion he had been convincing the Jews that they were safe in his keeping. He gave them false hopes. When Russia invades, he will turn out to be a hireling shepherd (Zechariah 11:15-17). The hireling thinks of nothing but his own skin. When the wolf (the northern aggressor) comes, the hireling (the Jewish antichrist) flees (John 10:12). He will hide out in his religious capital at Jerusalem or in his commercial capital at Babylon. He will leave the sheep (Israel) to fend for themselves. When the invaders have perished, he will come out of the woodwork and instigate more plans to elevate himself at Israel's expense.

The Scripture is everywhere consistent with itself on the subject of the northern army losing the war. God comforts Israel by telling her not to be afraid of the Assyrian even though this aggressor smites her, "for yet a little while, and the indignation shall cease, and mine anger in their [the Assyrians'] destruction" (Isaiah 10:24,25). The Lord promises to break the Assyrian in Israel and tread him underfoot upon the mountains (Isaiah 14:25). Repeatedly God states that He is against the northern leader (Ezekiel 38:3; 39:1). God Himself will enter into judgment against him with pestilence and blood. The king of the north will be broken without the aid of a human hand (Daniel 8:25). He will come to a sudden end with no one to help him (Daniel 11:45). God pledges to drive the northern army into a desolate and barren land, where the stench of rotting corpses will testify to Russia's inglorious defeat (Joel 2:20).

The defeat of the great northern power in answer to Israel's prayers is a commentary upon God's ability and desire to rescue His people from danger. When the enemy comes in like a flood, the Spirit of the Lord raises up a standard against the foe (Isaiah 59:19). This is the same God who even now is working to deliver us from the wrath to come (I Thessalonians 1:10) Each of us can say with the Apostle Paul that the Lord has delivered me out of the mouth of the lion, and He shall deliver me from every evil work and will preserve me unto his heavenly kingdom

(II Timothy 4:17,18).

Though Satan rage against us, we are safe in our Father's keeping. The Lord Jesus is a faithful shepherd. When danger lurks near, He does not desert His sheep. We are safe for time and eternity. He has given to us eternal life, and we shall never perish.

THE SHOWDOWN . . .

9

Western Europe
Enters the War

Western Europe
Enters the War

Shortly after the Russian troops have occupied North Africa, they will hear disturbing reports from the northeast (Daniel 11:44). We can conclude that the military dictator of Western Europe has at last come to the aid of Israel. Occupational forces from the West are beginning to move masses of men and machines into Palestine. Their intention is to cut the armies of the north off from the home base. After several decades of cold war, peaceful coexistence, and then detente, Europe finally is forced to face Russia in a military showdown.

Before examining the Biblical evidence for the arrival of the European armies, let us acquaint ourselves with the general situation in the West as it will be during the first half of the tribulation. At the beginning of the tribulation a consolidation of Europe will be in progress. For generations Bible teachers have been calling the consolidation "The Revived Roman Empire." Some students of prophecy object to this term, for they say elements of Roman law never disappeared from history and therefore did not die. Besides, they point out, the nations involved in the coming European consolidation may not correspond exactly to the territories of the ancient Roman empire.

Whether these scholars are right is not really crucial. Probably it is safest and more accurate to refer to the unification of Europe as "The Reorganized Roman Empire." Many are now calling it the United States of Europe. The unification of Europe will certainly be a redevelopment and a continuation of what commenced in the Roman empire, and the newly formed organization will operate on the same governmental principle that characterized old Rome.

The reality of Rome revived or reshaped is certain. The statue in Nebuchadnezzar's dream (Daniel 2) is a prophecy of the course of Gentile history. It covers the period from Nebuchadnezzar to the second coming of Christ. The head of gold represents the Babylonian empire under Nebuchadnezzar. The shoulders, chest, and arms of silver represent the Medo-Persian empire under Cyrus and Darius. The belly and thighs of bronze represent the Greek empire under Alexander. The legs of iron represent the Roman empire under the Caesars.

The ten toes of iron mixed with clay represent a further development of the Roman empire (Daniel 2:41). This ten-part development has never yet occurred in history. This ten-part development will exist at the second coming of Christ (Daniel 2:44). At the time when ten kings rule in the territories once held by Rome, Jesus Christ will set up His kingdom on earth. The Lord will not establish His kingdom until these ten kings emerge.

All of this information is repeated in a different way and with a different emphasis in Daniel 7. The lion represents the Babylonian empire. The bear represents the Medo-Persian empire. The leopard represents the Greek empire. The terrible beast represents the Roman empire. The ten horns on the terrible beast depict a further development of the Roman empire in which ten kings arise to rule the empire simultaneously. This development has never yet occurred. Never in the history of Rome did ten kings rule at the same time within the territories of Rome.

A new feature of the Roman empire appears in Daniel 7:8,20,24,25. An eleventh horn sprouts up after the ten horns are in place. This represents a ruler who will emerge within the territories of old Rome. He will have an insignificant beginning and only gradually arise to prominence. Three of the Western kings will oppose him, but he will manage to silence their opposition (Daniel 7:24).

Revelation 13 completes the picture. The beast with the ten horns and ten crowns is the reorganized Roman empire.

THE SHOWDOWN . . .

The great marvel is that the Roman empire should disappear from history as a recognizable government and then reappear as a ten-nation federation (Revelation 13:1). The emperor is none other than the little horn of Daniel 7.

In Revelation 13:5 we learn that the emperor-dictator continues in a position of absolute power for forty-two months. The European dictator, then, does not arise to power until the middle of the tribulation period. His activities are confined to the last three and one-half years of the tribulation. Then in Revelation 17:12,13, another factor contributes to our knowledge of the redevelopment of the Roman empire. The ten kings of Europe agree to grant the eleventh king dictatorial power.

When you have all this information at hand, you will see that the future form of the Roman empire develops in three stages: (1) in the beginning of the tribulation—the rise of ten kings who rule simultaneously over territories within the general boundaries of old Rome; (2) in the middle of the tribulation, the emergence of the European dictator to whom the ten kings consent to give absolute authority; (3) the uncontested rule of the emperor.

The third stage in the development of the coming empire is made possible by the destruction of Russia. The number one threat to European economy and safety suddenly melts away when Russia perishes in the Middle East. With the removal of Russia, the European emperor can concentrate upon pursuing his own interests unhindered (Revelation 13:4). In collaboration with the Jewish antichrist in Palestine, the European dictator will control all of the territory from the Atlantic to the Persian Gulf.

Russia's invasion of the Middle East brings the armies of Europe to Israel. Russia's sudden destruction by meteorological phenomena makes a confrontation between the European dictator and the Russian destroyer unnecessary. The absence of Russia as a world-power gives the European dictator on occasion for filling the vacuum.

Now let us look at the evidence which indicates that the Western powers will be present in the Middle Eat. Revelation 11:2 predicts that the city of Jerusalem will be under Gentile control for forty-two months—the last three and one-half years of the tribulation. The same chapter describes the death of two witnesses in Jerusalem (verse 7). The beast (the European dictator) is responsible for their death. Furthermore, the beast makes war against the saints (Daniel 7:21; Revelation 13:7). The saints Daniel has in mind are Jewish believers who have returned to Palestine. Just a soon as the forces of the West arrive in Palestine, the emperor turns his attention to liquidating Jewish believers.

The destruction of Russia is only the beginning of Israel's problems (Isaiah 14:29). The enemy from without can no longer threaten her, but the enemy from within (the European dictator and his colleague the Jewish antichrist) present a grave new danger.

We can show from historical analogy that the forces of the West will occupy Palestine. Daniel predicted the activities of Antiochus Epiphanes (Antiochus IV, Epiphanes, 175—164 B.C., the ancient king of the north) centuries before their fulfillment. Beginning with verse 21 of chapter 11, Daniel described the expedition of Antiochus through Palestine to Egypt. While Antiochus was planning to subdue Egypt, Rome dispatched a navy to interfere with Antiochus' ambitions (Daniel 11:29.30). Rome's intervention so angered Antiochus that he vowed to wreak his vengeance upon Israel. But Roman forces stood up once more; and, according to Daniel, Rome polluted the Sanctuary in Jerusalem (verse 31).

This sequence in Daniel 11:29-31 precedes the prophecy in 11:40-45 about the last great king of the north (Russia) who will do the same thing Antiochus did and have the same results because of Western interference. Russia will invade Egypt. The Western powers will object to Russia's intentions to control the Middle East (Ezekiel 38:13). The Western powers will send a navy into the area. Russia will retreat to Jerusalem, intending to annihilate Jews (Daniel 11:44). God will destroy the Russian armies. The forces of the West will assert their jurisdiction over Palestine (Revelation 11:2). The European dictator will desecrate the Temple by stationing soldiers in the sacred precincts.

Another hint of the Western invasion occurs in Matthew 24:28: "For wheresoever the carcase is, there will the eagles be gathered together." This strange verse comes in a passage that deals with events immediately after the middle of the tribulation. The statue of the European dictator goes up in the Temple (verse 15). This is the signal which alerts Jews that the Russian invasion will occur immediately. Jews flee the land and remain in their hiding places until the Russian invaders are no longer a threat (verse 16).

The carcass of verse 28 represents the destroyed Russian army, lying on the mountains of Israel and in the wilderness of Judea. The carcass will draw the eagles (Revelation 8:13; read "eagle" for "angel"). The eagles represent the Western armies. An eagle was the insignia of Rome. The Roman empire of the future will make its presence and power felt in the Middle East at about the same time that Russia meets her doom in the Middle East.

Now if all the preceding information seems farfetched, consider a conclusive proof that the armies of the West will invade Palestine and participate ultimately in Armageddon. When the Lord Jesus comes to earth with the armies of Heaven, He will descend to Jerusalem, where He will execute the beast (the European dictator) and the false prophet (the Jewish antichrist) (Zechariah 14:4; Revelation 19:11-16,20). The beast and his armies gather at Megiddo, and here they will meet their doom by the personal appearance of Christ (Revelation 16:14-16).

Verse 2 of Zechariah 14 predicts that the Lord will gather all nations against Jerusalem to battle. The city will be captured, the residents will experience awful atrocities, and then the Lord will rush to Israel's defense. His feet will rest upon Olivet, and the armies which worked such ruination upon the people and city will suffer His withering blast. "All nations" certainly would include the armies of the West.

From the middle of the tribulation period to the end of it—forty-two months—the influence and control of the Western powers will be felt in the Middle East. As soon as the Western emperor gets dictatorial authority from the ten kings of Europe, he will order a statue of himself to be placed in the Jewish Temple. His colleague, the Jewish antichrist, will sit in the Temple (II Thessalonians 2:3-10), posing as Israel's king-priest and directing the nation in the worship of the Western emperor (Revelation 13:13-15).

Jerusalem has been under Gentile control to some extent since the first invasion of Nebuchadnezzar in 605 B.C. For forty-two months of the tribulation Jerusalem will be downtrodden by Gentiles in a fresh exhibition of Gentile control. That control will continue until Christ breaks the back of Gentile dominion. He will smite the Gentiles in the final stage of Armageddon at Megiddo.

The present status of Jerusalem, under Jewish control for the first time in many centuries, is only temporary. And this is not control in any absolute sense. Jews now govern Jerusalem only by Gentile consent. Then too, Jews have not taken possession of the Temple site. This site still remains in Arab hands.

God has destined that Israel will be restored to sovereign power. He plans to restore the kingdom of David. The fulfillment of these plans necessitates putting an end to Gentile political supremacy. The times of the Gentiles (Luke 21:24) will end at the last stage of the war of Armageddon, when East and West assemble for a battle that will decide which one will dominate the earth and both will suffer total extinction by a blast of Christ's almighty power.

All of the details of prophecy serve to teach us that our sovereign God has everything under His control. He manipulates the nations as He pleases. He interferes with their wicked plans or uses their evil designs for the purpose of working out His own plans.

The same is true with the Lord's interventions in our

lives. He overrules our plans and causes them to serve His purpose. He works all things together for our good. Even the enemies who assail us will further His design to exalt us in due season. Nothing that we experience just happens by accident. Everything—however frustrating and fearful—contributes to an overall scheme. God knows the end from the beginning and He is working toward a glorious goal.

10

The Far East
Mobilizes for War

The Far East
Mobilizes for War

Armageddon will involve much more than a single battle. As we have already seen, Armageddon is a war that continues for most of the last half of the tribulation. Armageddon includes a series of military campaigns which will climax at Megiddo.

Four invasions will be a part of this final war: (1) North Africa, spearheaded by Egypt, will invade northward into Israel; (2) Russia, assisted by a growing army, will invade southward into Israel and penetrate to North Africa; (3) Western Europe, under the dictatorship of the little horn, will invade eastward into Israel in order to fill the vacancy left by Russia and the collapse of the Arab world; (4) the kings of Asia will invade westward into Israel.

Revelation 16:12 contains the clearest reference to an invasion from the Orient. The sixth vial or bowl judgment strikes the Euphrates River and dries it up so that "the way of the kings of the east might be prepared." The kings of the east, or kings of the sunrise, are undoubtedly hordes of invaders from China, India, Korea, and other Asiatic nations.

The existence of a federation of nations from the East which obviously makes an attack upon the Middle East—a Middle East under the control of Western armies—has some interesting implications. For one thing, a hostile concentration of powers in the Orient shows you that neither the European dictator nor his colleague the Jewish antichrist ever rise to absolute global mastery during the tribulation. They never gain political or military control over China, Japan, and the other nations of the Far East. Their control is more or less confined to the Roman world, the territories which touch the Mediterranean Sea.

The coming United States of Europe will extend its political and military jurisdiction to the Middle East after the destruction of Russia and her allies. North Africa will come under the umbrella of the United States of Europe after Russia's collapse. Just what part the United States of America and the other countries in the Western Hemisphere will have in the United States of Europe is a question that puzzles most Bible teachers. But one thing is certain— the United States of Europe will not dominate the Orient. The West may have a powerful economic and commercial influence on the entire planet, but the European dictator is not a world dictator in an absolute sense.

The same was true of the world dictators of the past. Nebuchadnezzar certainly did not hold sway over the North American Indians. The Caesars were all world dictators, but they did not rule Persia, India, China, etc. They ruled the *oikoumene,* the civilized world in contrast to the world of barbarians who lived outside the Roman empire.

Barbarian invasions from beyond the boundaries of the Roman empire brought an end to Rome, and a future barbaric invasion from the territories outside the reorganized Roman empire will devastate the kingdom of the beast, the European dictator.

What prompts the combined armies of the Orient to march on the Middle East? The Scripture gives us some hints, and we can make some suggestions without dogmatism. A devilish motivation lies behind the eastern invaders. The filthy demons who inspire the activities of the European dictator and his Jewish associate will abandon these two leaders at some point toward the end of the tribulation (Revelation 16:13,14). The demon powers will concentrate upon the Asiatic leaders, enticing them to Palestine. The kings of the whole world will assemble in Palestine at the instigation of infernal influences.

The Oriental kings, of course, will have their own reasons for invading the Middle East. Chinese Communism has resolved to rule the world. Russia's defeat will give China

85

new incentive. The presence of the European dictator and his armies in Palestine is reason enough for China to take counteraction. China knows that the power which rules the Middle East is the power that controls the world. China will make a bid for that place of absolute dominion.

The activities of the European dictator and the Jewish antichrist will obviously be a growing threat to China's interests. Remember that the two colleagues in crime engage in two enterprises either of which is enough to disgust the Chinese leaders. In the middle of the tribulation period the European dictator will destroy the ecumenical church and substitute emperor worship (Revelation 17:16-18). China will not tolerate the deification of a Western leader, especially in view of the fact that China recognizes the deity of its own leader. Rival gods will vie for supremacy.

Besides aiming to control religion, the Jewish antichrist will work to control world commerce (Revelation 13:16,17). It looks very much as though he will establish his religious capital at Jerusalem and his commercial capital at Babylon. A restored city of Babylon on the Euphrates River will become a marketplace for the nations.

Even though China will not experience political and military subjugation to the rising Western empire, it cannot help being seriously endangered by economic monopolies in the West. And then, what happens when the Jewish antichrist refuses to trade with the Orient until its peoples bear the image of the beast in their foreheads or hands? Don't expect China to take such an ultimatum sitting down. The sleeping giant will arise and attack. She will think it past time to contest the growing power of the Western empire and assert her own claims for world rule.

In the waning hours of the tribulation a disaster will strike the Euphrates River. The water will dry up, and the Asiatic armies will march in the dry riverbed all the way to northeastern Palestine (Revelation 16:12). From there it will be no trouble to aim the army toward the Valley of Megiddo and confront the Western allies.

The drying up of Euphrates is an interesting subject. The sixth vial of judgment accomplishes this feat. The first five vial judgments of Revelation 16 have to do specifically with the kingdom of the beast (the reorganized Roman empire). These judgments inflict terrible suffering upon the people who live in the empire. The judgment causes death on an unprecedented scale.

Is it not possible that God will use the Asiatic powers as His instrument of judgment? You can see how China might bombard Europe and the Middle East with atomic warheads which would wipe out every major city, including Babylon (verse 19). The intense heat which will accompany the destruction of the beast's empire certainly suggests nuclear warfare or something worse (verses 8,9). God employed an Oriental army to destroy the power of Babylon in the past, and Scripture gives us reason to think He will command a repeat performance in the time of the end.

The times of the Gentiles commenced when Nebuchadnezzar invaded Jerusalem. He was the first Gentile monarch to tread the Holy City under his feet. Nebuchadnezzar erected an image of himself and commanded his subjects to worship it (Daniel 3:1-7). In these respects—and in many more—he is the exact counterpart of the last Gentile dictator (the European dictator). When God put into effect His plan to end Babylonian power, He raised up an army from the east of the Euphrates, He brought the Persians against Babylon.

The story of the fall of ancient Babylon is interesting as well as prophetic. Many months prior to the siege Cyrus engaged his troops in digging a divisionary canal off from the Euphrates out of the sight of Babylon. The Euphrates ran through Babylon in its southward course toward the Persian Gulf. At the right moment Cyrus redirected the flow of the Euphrates either out into a huge lake or else around Babylon and back into the river channel below the city (Isaiah 44:27—45:3). The part of the river that flowed through the city was empty of water. Cyrus marched his Persian troops on the dry channel underneath the walls of the city. Babylon surrendered, and the Babylonian empire came to an end (Daniel 5:30, 31).

The victory over ancient Babylon by an army that came from a land remotely to the east of the Euphrates was prophesied frequently. Isaiah spoke of the eastern army as "the noise of a multitude in the mountains, like as of a great people; a tumultous noise of the kingdoms of nations gathered together: the Lord of hosts mustereth the host of the battle. They come from a far country, from the end of heaven . . ." (Isaiah 13:4,5).

According to prophecy, when the eastern army destroys Babylon, the city will never afterward have a single inhabitant (verse 20). This did not happen when Cyrus conquered Babylon. The complete destruction of the city awaits a future rebuilding and a future destruction by another army from the Far East. The prophecies which describe the utter and absolute destruction of Babylon will be fulfilled at the very end of the tribulation (verses 9-11), when the Oriental armies will prepare for a massive invasion by destroying the cities and defense installations of the West.

When the territory of the beast lies in smoldering ruins, the eastern attackers will follow up their aerial bombardment with the mobilization of the infantry. They will pour into Palestine by following the Fertile Crescent northwest from Babylon to Syria and then by descending upon the Plain of Esdraelon from the northeast.

Hearing that the armies of the Orient are moving toward Palestine, the armies of the West dig in at the site of ancient Megiddo for the attack. The loss of Babylon, Jerusalem, and other great cities of the empire is a disaster of unparalleled proportions. The West determines to make a last stand and fight for its survival.

Whether the two enormous armies ever actually fight each other is open to conjecture. We do know the outcome, however. The Lord Jesus Christ will suddenly rend the sky. He will come with the armies of Heaven to smite the assembled armies with the sword that proceeds from His mouth (Revelation 19:11-15). He will give full expression to His undiluted wrath. The carcasses of the slain will provide a gruesome banquet for the vultures (verses 17,18).

Christ will deal with the beast (the European dictator) and all the kings who have allied themselves with him (verse 20). He will cast the beast and the false prophet (the Jewish antichrist) directly into Gehenna — the lake of fire. The Lord will also slay the rest of the armies (the Oriental armies) and give their carcasses to the birds of prey (verse 21). When Christ finishes His destructive work, not one unsaved person will be left alive in the whole area.

The Lord Jesus will restore the Davidic dynasty by ruling upon the throne of Israel as David's promised heir. His rule will commence in the land of Israel and for a thousand years gradually extend its dominion until the whole earth recognizes His supremacy and bows to His authority.

During the kingdom reign of Christ, Gentile domination over Israel will cease forever. Israel will become a nation of priests who render acceptable service to God. The Gentiles will serve Israel. Our prayer will at last be answered: "[Let] thy kingdom come; [let] thy will be done on earth as it is in heaven."

The kingdom of Messiah will dawn in history after the night of Armageddon. The shadows are now lengthening. Armageddon looms ahead as a dark and sinister reality.

Jesus said that when we see these events beginning to take shape, we should realize that His coming is near, even at the doors (Luke 21:28). Never before in history has such an accumulation of indications pointed to the speedy return of Christ. All of the nations that will be involved in Armageddon are continuously in the news. Israel is a nation. The Arab nations are seething with rage against Israel.

Russia is maneuvering to control the Middle East without getting involved in a shootout with the members of the North Atlantic Treaty Organization. China is already supplying arms to Mideast revolutionaries. The success of a United States of Europe is a greater prospect now than ever before, for Europe is feverishly working to eclipse the United States in economic power by destroying the dollar.

All of these conditions are a necessary preparation for the fulfillment of prophecy. The day of Christ's appearing is at hand. That being true, let us who are Christians awake out of sleep; for now is our salvation nearer than when first we believed (Romans 13:11).

If you are not a Christian, won't you recognize that ours may be the generation that will witness Armageddon's gory confrontation? What this should convey to you is a determination to accept the gracious counsel of God to trust in His Son and be saved from sin and judgment (Romans 5:8,9). Don't let the opportunity slip through your fingers; it may pass suddenly (II Corinthians 6:2b; Proverbs 27:1). With Christ as your Saviour Heaven will be your prospect, and you can be sure that the rumblings of Armageddon will not reach that peaceful place.

11

Days of Glory
for History

Days of Glory
for History

An interesting question has captured the attention of certain philosophers. They ask, Does history have any meaning or follow any pattern? They want to know whether each and every event in history belongs to some overall plan. In other words, does history have a purpose. Men who think about such matters suggest a variety of answers.

Some hold the opinion that history has no pattern or meaning; everything that happens is the result of blind coincidence. They say no plan or purpose is discernible in history. It is aimless and haphazard.

Others contend that history endlessly repeats itself. They argue that history moves in cycles. It goes round and round without getting anywhere. Whatever happens to man will happen again and again—forever.

A third group of philosophers defend the view that history has a goal and that it is moving purposefully in a predesigned direction. History is going someplace, and all of the seeming contradictions and paradoxes fit into an intelligent plan. They declare that nothing occurs by chance or at random. Every event is a significant part of a larger scheme.

The last view, of course, is the teaching of the Bible. Perhaps no verse of Scripture puts the truth more succinctly than Ephesians 1:9,10: "Having made known unto us the mystery of his will, according to his good pleasure which he hath purposed in himself; that in the dispensation of the fulness of time he might gather together in one all things in Christ, both which are in heaven, and which are on earth; even in him."

This complicated passage explains that all things are moving purposefully toward one climactic era in which Christ will figure as the Lord of history. History will reach its grand consummation at a time when Christ unites Heaven and earth under one government and brings earth into harmony with Heaven. This concept of the meaning of history is not the product of human speculation; it is the product of divine revelation. God has made known this mystery.

It is God's good pleasure and eternal purpose to bring everything and everyone under the sovereignty of His Son. Everything that has ever occurred in human history or that will ever occur in the future somehow relates to this eternal purpose of making Christ the Lord of history. The Father has purposed that every knee will bow to the Lord Jesus Christ and that every tongue will confess that He is Lord (Philippians 2:10,11).

Rebels against God repudiated and blasphemed Christ in time and in history past and present. But you can be confident that God will vindicate His Son in time and in history future. Historical circumstances surrounded His rejection; historical circumstances will surround His ultimate exaltation. History was the context of His redemptive work, and history will be the context of His Messianic work. As history was the witness of His sufferings, so shall history become the witness of His glory.

As a thoughtful Christian you would not disagree with the necessity for and the actuality of a historical vindication of the Lord Jesus Christ, would you? Just what form that historical vindication will take has divided the Bible-believing world into rival camps.

Perhaps the majority of Christians hold the view that the historical vindication will be brief. They teach that world conditions will continue to worsen until Christ intervenes by His promised appearing. At that moment, so they say, He will return to earth and bring a sudden finale to history. With that the eternal state will commence immediately. This is the view of the amillennialists, those who do not believe in a literal 1,000-year reign of Christ on Planet Earth.

Another large company of Christians embrace the view that the historical vindication of Christ will require a thousand years. They maintain that world conditions will continue to deteriorate until Christ intervenes. At that time He will rectify political, social, economic, and ecclesiastical wrongs and preserve peace, justice, and prosperity for a thousand years. This is the view of the premillennialists.

A much smaller group of Christians see a third outcome of history. They believe the preaching of the gospel and the influence of Christianity will gradually bring about an improvement of world conditions; and when at last man has succeeded in conquering disease, solving racial tensions, banishing war, and providing equal opportunities for all, Christ will return to earth and usher in the eternal state. This is the view of the postmillennialists.

The amillennialist's view of the outcome of history is totally pessimistic. His only hope for the triumph of good over evil lies beyond human history in eternity. He sees nothing but failure, struggle, catastrophes, and chaos as long as history endures. He interprets history to be only a segment of time between eternity past and eternity future in which God is saving His elect people. Throughout history God is executing His redemptive program. History has only soteriological (salvation) significance for the amillennialists. This view disappoints every human expectation for a better and brighter day in the course of history. It offers no prospect of a Golden Age.

The postmillennial view is greatly optimistic. It sees for the most part steady progress ahead. It believes the gospel will Christianize the nations. It thinks the church, civilization, social agencies, science, and politics are the means God is using to achieve spiritual progress and the ultimate victory of the kingdom of God. This view disappoints any realist. Who can believe the postmillennial interpretation when we observe all around us contradictory facts?

The world is not getting better. Moral corruption increases hourly. Social injustices continue unabated. Bigotry and hatred abound. Lawlessness and revolution prevail. The only real advances occur in scientific technology. But even here the solution of one problem gives rise to a more complicated one.

Besides all that, we have Biblical warrent for believing that neither the gospel nor the church will Christianize the world. Evil men and seducers will wax worse and worse (II Timothy 3:13). War, pestilence, earthquakes, sorrows, martyrdoms, false teaching, and anarchy will continue until Jesus returns (Matthew 24:6-12). The Lord Jesus once asked the question, "When the Son of man cometh, will he find faith on the earth?" Does this sound as if conditions of spirituality will characterize the end of the age?

The premillennial view manifests a pessimistic optimism. Examine it and you will find that it agrees with the amillennialist in holding a pessimistic outlook toward man's schemes to effect lasting peace. It takes seriously those passages of Scripture which explain that earth's darkest day lies ahead. On the other hand, the premillennial view exhibits a healthy optimism about the ultimate outcome of history. Like the postmillennialist, the premillennialist anticipates a time of political, social, economic, scientific, environmental, material, and physical progress. The dream of humanity for a better world will surely come to pass in history. Doesn't that make you want to praise the Lord?

Premillennialism is pessimistic about the outcome of the church age, but it is optimistic about the outcome of history, for it believes the coming of Christ will introduce a Golden Age of history—the dispensation of the fullness of time. It maintains that all history has been moving toward this final epoch in history in which Christ will solve every human dilemma and restore Planet Earth to Edenic beauty, productivity, and harmony. This is the millennial hope.

We might ask at this point, What is the basis for such a hope? What reason have we for entertaining such a prospect? We need something more than an optimistic philosophy of history to undergird this hope.

The premillennial view of the goal of history is the view of the Old Testament prophets. Check these Bible verses for yourself.

Isaiah 2:4 envisions a time of international peace under the administration of Israel's Messiah.

Isaiah 9:6,7 anticipates the increase and perpetuity of the Davidic government as executed by the divine Son.

Isaiah 11:3-5 predicts the triumph of righteousness, equity, and justice.

Isaiah 11:6-8 pictures the return of Edenic conditions among brute creatures.

Isaiah 35:1,2 describes the reclamation of desert wastes.

Isaiah 35:5,6 anticipates a time when physical defects will be nonexistent.

Isaiah 60:1-5 looks forward to the salvation of the Gentiles on a universal scale.

It is easy to duplicate these prospects in all of the prophets. The point is, the Old Testament prophets held a view of history which looked to the coming of the Messiah as the only solution to the present crises and chaos. At His coming they believed He would elevate Israel to political supremacy over the nations; He would restore the social order; He would introduce ecclesiastical changes; He would dispense equal justice. And He would initiate a lasting peace and prosperity.

Even amillennial scholars admit that a literal interpretation of the prophets leads to this conclusion. Amillennialism, however, rejects the literal method of interpretation when it comes to matters concerning the second coming of Christ. Amillennialists allegorize or mysticalize the prophecies. In other words, they do not believe Isaiah's reference to the lion lying down with the lamb means that a literal lion will literally lie down beside a literal lamb without literally any desire to kill and eat the lamb. Rather, they see in this reference only a mystical meaning—namely, the time will come in the gospel era when God's grace will take the beastly impulses out of man.

The whole issue between the premillennialist and the amillennialist boils down to this: shall we interpret the prophecies literally or mystically? Premillennialism rests upon a literal interpretation of Scripture. Amillennialism rests upon a mystical interpretation. Premillennialists teach that the Old Testament prophets looked for a literal Messianic prince to sit upon a literal throne in the literal city of Jerusalem for the purpose of enforcing a literal peace and a literal righteousness upon a literal Israel and upon literal nations.

Didn't Mary, the mother of Jesus, interpret the prophets literally? Gabriel had announced to her that she would bear a child who would sit upon the throne of David and reign over the house of Israel (Luke 1:31-33). You can be certain that Mary anticipated much more than a new era of spiritual blessings, ethical salvation, and the outreaching of divine mercy (Luke 1:47-50); she also anticipated social, political, and material changes (Luke 1:51-53).

Mary regarded the approaching day of Messiah as the fulfillment of the Abrahamic Covenant. That Covenant guaranteed to Israel both material and spiritual blessings forever. The spiritual blessings included justification; the material blessings included possession of the land of Canaan forever.

Zacharias, the father of John the Baptist, obviously interpreted the prophets literally. His encounter with Gabriel and the subsequent birth of John had convinced Zacharias that the Abrahamic Covenant was about to be fulfilled. Zacharias understood the spiritual implications of the Covenant, for he spoke of holiness, righteousness, and remission of sins (Luke 1:75,77). But he also had something to say about the national, material, and physical implications of the Covenant, for he expected a national deliverance from political enemies (Luke 1:71,74). Until Israel enjoys such a deliverance, the promise of God to Abraham remains unfulfilled.

The New Testament disciples shared the same hope that animated the prophets. Moreover, they interpreted the teachings of Jesus in this light. Of course, the amillennialist says that the disciples' hope for the establishment of a literal politico-social kingdom was a "carnal expectation." The amillennialist believes the disciples misunderstood Jesus. He thinks that all of Jesus' references to the kingdom pertained only to a spiritual role of Christ in the believer's heart.

Don't you agree that it is pretty difficult, if not impossible, to harmonize the amillennial view with Matthew 19:28? In this passage Jesus promised the disciples that they would sit upon twelve thrones, judging the twelve tribes of Israel at the time of the regeneration and at the time when the Son of Man would sit upon the throne of His glory. If the expectation of the disciples for a literal kingdom was carnal, as the amillennialist says, then Jesus certainly pandered to their carnal expectation by assuring each of them a place of governmental authority over Israel. This passage confirms their expectation by promising a new social order in which the disciples would figure as administrators.

After the years of our Lord's public teaching, after His death and resurrection, and after another forty days of instruction about the kingdom, the disciples asked the Lord whether it was now time for Him to restore the kingdom to Israel (Acts 1:6). The death and resurrection of Christ and their own unusual enduement with the Holy Spirit (John 20:22) had not altered their so-called "carnal expectation." Indeed, they must have looked upon the resurrection as a final proof that Jesus was the Messiah and therefore fully qualified and ready to introduce the promised kingdom.

If the kingdom had already come, the disciples were unaware of it. If the kingdom was simply the sovereign rule of Christ in the believer's heart, the disciples certainly were unfamiliar with this interpretation of the kingdom. They thought that nothing now stood in the way of inaugurating the kingdom that the prophets had foretold, that John the Baptist had announced, and that Jesus had frequently said was "at hand."

There was no better moment for the Lord to explain to these disciples once and for all that they had misconstrued everything He had ever said about the kingdom. Why did not He say, "The kingdom has already come in the sense that the redemptive work of the Messiah has already begun and in the sense that you disciples have bowed your knee to my sovereign will"? Instead of setting them straight, the Lord merely told the disciples that the time for the restoration of the kingdom to Israel belonged to the secret plan and will of the Father. It was not a question of *whether* the kingdom would dawn as the prophets had predicted but *when* the kingdom would dawn. From the human point of view, it is only the time element about the restored kingdom that is uncertain.

In preaching to the men of Israel, the Apostle Peter declared that if the nation would repent of their sins, the times of refreshing would come and God would send Jesus back to Israel (Acts 3:19-21). The times of refreshing and the times of restitution in these verses are synonymous with the consolation of Israel (Luke 2:25), the redemption in Jerusalem (Luke 2:38), and the kingdom of God (Luke 23:51).

The restitution refers to the restoration of Israel to her land in Palestine in fulfillment of the Palestinian Covenant and the restoration of the theocracy (God's direct rule over the nation) in Israel in fulfillment of the Davidic Covenant. This restitution is exactly what all of the prophets had predicted (Acts 3:21).

Study the public ministry of Christ and you will discover that Christ gave His disciples a little foretaste of kingdom conditions. The miracles He performed would certainly confirm the disciples in their anticipation of a literal fulfillment of the Old Testament prophecies. He miraculously fed the hungry, cured the ailing, controlled the elements, and raised the dead, just as the prophets literally anticipated. He provided physically, materially, socially, and economically for His people as well as spiritually.

Will anyone argue that Jesus' three-year ministry fulfilled in full all of the material benefits which the prophets associated with the Golden Age of history? Hardly! In the ministry of Christ on earth we catch a glimpse of what kingdom conditions will be, but Jesus ministered to only a handful of people. Millions were left to suffer in their physical distresses and to die. He did nothing to reverse the political misfortunes of Israel.

The prophets, however, anticipated on a universal scale freedom from disease, distress, death, destitution, demons, and defects. They longed for Messiah to usher in the age which would finally give meaning to history and at last terminate the historical process.

We who are premillennialists are still looking for Christ to introduce this age—the millennial kingdom. Only then will God fulfill in full all of the implications of the covenants. Only then will history come to a reasonable and satisfying conclusion. Only then will Christ demonstrate that He is the Lord of history and the architect of the ages as well as the sovereign of eternity.

12

Getting Ready for
the Reign of Christ

Getting Ready for
the Reign of Christ

The Old Testament prophets saw the kingdom in the distant future. The fulfillment would come in the last days or after many days (Hosea 3:4,5; Isaiah 2:2). It belonged to the time of the end. John the Baptist and Jesus brought it out of the remote future by announcing, "The kingdom is at hand." The time for fulfillment had come (Mark 1:14,15). But the actual establishment of the kingdom depended upon the spiritual preparedness of Israel as a nation. God would not and will not restore the Davidic kingdom to a rebellious and apostate Israel.

The attitude of the nation toward the Lord Jesus Christ demonstrated how ill-prepared Israel was to participate in Messiah's kingdom. The representatives of the people officially rejected the Messiah, with the result that Jesus withdrew the proffer of the kingdom. The kingdom is no longer at hand. It is not now imminent. The kingdom program has entered a state of suspension while God is working out His eternal plans for the church.

Israel's repudiation and crucifixion of her Messiah was necessary to the kingdom program. The prophets everywhere take for granted that the citizens of the kingdom will be redeemed subjects of the King. Without the atoning work of Christ no one would qualify spiritually for participating in the kingdom reign. Forgiveness of sin is an integral part of the kingdom (Jeremiah 31:34; Isaiah 55:7), and the death of Christ is an indispensable factor in providing that forgiveness.

When the church age comes to a close at the rapture (the event in which Christ comes in the air to catch away the church from the earth), the kingdom program will resume.

God will raise up 144,000 Jewish evangelists who will announce the imminence of Messiah's kingdom (Matthew 24:14; Revelation 7:2-8). The judgments of the tribulation period are designed to produce a purged and purified Israel to whom God will fulfill the promises He made to Abraham and David by covenant oath.

Unlike Israel's attitude at the first coming of Christ, at His second coming the nation will officially and formally give Him a royal welcome (Matthew 23:39). A regenerate and reconciled nation will receive the King and participate in the glories of His earthly reign.

The time for the inauguration of the kingdom is at present indefinite, for we do not know how long the church age will continue. From the rapture of the church to the introduction of the kingdom the time is more definite; at least seven years intervene. Nevertheless, enough uncertainty remains that the Lord exhorts the tribulation saints to watch daily for His return to establish the kingdom. No one can calculate the day or the hour of this tremendous event (Matthew 25:13).

As the tribulation saints see the signs of the times multiplying, they will know that the time for kingdom manifestation is drawing nearer and nearer (Matthew 24:15-21,33). The judgments of the "great tribulation" period must run their appointed course of exactly 1,260 days, the last three and a half years of the tribulation (Daniel 7:25; Revelation 11:2,3; 12:14; 13:5).

At the end of these days the European dictator, the Jewish deceiver, and all of their armies will meet their doom by the return of the Lord Jesus to the earth (Revelation 19:20). In that day His feet will touch down upon the Mount of Olives (Zechariah 14:4). He will begin the process of preparing for a formal inauguration of kingdom conditions.

A very short interval will occur between the end of the tribulation and the beginning of the millennial age. The prophet Daniel puts a period of seventy-five days between these two events (Daniel 12:11,12). We cannot dogmatize about the purpose of these intervening days, but in all likelihood the following events will transpire at this time: (1) the resurrection of Old Testament saints and tribulation martyrs; (2) the cleansing of the land from the carnage of war; (3) the judgment of Israel and the nations; (4) the return of dispersed Jews to Palestine; and (5) the celebration of the feast of tabernacles. Let us have a look at each of these events.

The resurrection of Old Testament saints and tribulation martyrs. At the end of the tribulation and before the inauguration of the millennial kingdom the Lord will raise from the dead the Old Testament saints and the tribulation martyrs (John 5:25,29; Revelation 20:4,6). None of these will forfeit participation in the kingdom because of death. Isaiah 25:8 promises that the Messiah "will swallow up death in victory." Isaiah 26:19 assures Israel that her dead "shall live." This resurrection follows a time when the nation has suffered the anguish of birth pangs (the tribulation period—Isaiah 26:16-18).

Daniel 12:2 describes the same resurrection. Righteous Jews will awake from among the sleepers of the dust and enter into the life of the kingdom. The chronology of Daniel 12:1,2 is obvious: verse 1 describes the great tribulation; verse 2 anticipates a resurrection after the tribulation passes.

When the Lord Jesus raised Jairus' daughter, the widow of Nain's son, and Lazarus, the disciples would certainly associate these resurrections with the miracles of and preparation for the kingdom age. They would conclude that these people were raised from the dead in order to participate in the Messiah's reign—and doubtlessly they would have participated if the kingdom had not been deferred to another time period.

The cleansing of the land from the carnage of war. The destruction of Russia and her satellite forces upon the mountains of Israel will produce a pollution that will require seven months to bury the dead and another seven years to burn the implements of war (Ezekiel 39:9,12). The annihilation of the armies of the beast (the political leader of the revived Roman Empire) and the Oriental armies will result in more contamination. Before the Lord officially inaugurates the kingdom reign, He will commission His servants to remove the rubble of war—if not from the entire land at least from the vicinity of the capital city. During the millennial reign the cleaning-up operations will continue in the outlying districts of the Mid East (Ezekiel 39:14,15).

The judgment of Israel and the nations. The holocaust of the tribulation judgments will devastate the land and depopulate the cities (Joel 2:3; Revelation 16:19). Thousands will perish. Many rebel Jews and Gentiles will die in the various calamities and invasions. When Christ returns to earth, He will deal with those rebels who survive the tribulation catastrophes. He will slay unsaved Jews and Gentiles with the blast of His nostrils (II Thessalonians 1:7-9). Think of it, at the time He inaugurates the kingdom, there will be no unregenerate people living in Immanuel's land!

The return of dispersed Jews to Palestine. It will take some time to regather dispersed Jews to the land of Palestine. Christ will not inaugurate the kingdom until every last one of them has returned from the ends of the earth (Isaiah 27:12,13; Ezekiel 39:28). Isaiah pictures these people coming from such remote places as China (Isaiah 49:12). He sees Gentile kings assisting the weary travelers (verse 22; Isaiah 60:9). He depicts them as walking back to Palestine over highways that have been prepared for them (Isaiah 11:16; 19:23; 35:8).

The celebration of the feast of tabernacles. Finally, regathered Israel will have to wait for the arrival of the feast of tabernacles in October. In all probability the celebration of this feast will mark the official commencement of the millennial age. It may be that on this occasion the promises of Joel 2:28,29 will be fulfilled. The commencement of the church age was signaled by an unprecedented movement of the Holy Spirit, and we may suppose that unique manifestations of the Spirit's power will signal the beginning of the millennial reign.

All that we have said about the introduction of the millennial kingdom presupposes that the kingdom is a literal, 1,000-year reign over literal subjects. It is a historical kingdom. It is the rule of Heaven come down to earth. Christ will introduce a new regime in time and history. The empire which He will manage is just as literal, historical, visible, material, political, social, economical, and physical as the empire of the Caesars. In fact, the fifth and final world empire (the kingdom of Christ) will replace a succession of four world empires: the Babylonian empire, the Medo-Persian empire, the Greek empire, and the Roman empire. A Roman empire reorganized as a ten-nation unit will dominate the Mediterranean world just before Jesus comes (Daniel 2:44). The kingdom of Christ will follow the kingdom of the beast.

A kingdom includes a realm, a ruler, and subjects who comply with the regulations of the realm. It is appropriate now for us to inquire who the subjects are, where they come from, and what qualifies them for becoming kingdom citizens.

The charter citizens of the millennial reign are the regenerate Jews and Gentiles who survive the tribulation calamities (Revelation 7:4, 9-17). These saints have not been raised from the dead and have not been glorified. Sometime during the tribulation period they trusted Christ for the saving of their soul; they experienced the new birth. They lived through the tribulation (Matthew 24:13). The afflictions which they suffered purified their faith and inspired their hope (Daniel 12:10; Isaiah 48:10). They were alive to see the King coming in His glory with all His holy angels.

These charter citizens of the millennial reign (Revelation 7:14) will enter the age of millennial blessedness in their unglorified state. They will produce children and carry out all of the normal functions of this present life.

The essential qualification for participation in the kingdom age is regeneration. Jesus explained to Nicodemus that unless he was born of the Spirit, he would not live to see the kingdom and would not enter into it (John 3:3,5). Without the experience of the new birth and the subsequent sanctifying ministry of the Holy Spirit no one could measure up even in part to the spiritual requirements of the kingdom. The Sermon on the Mount expressly sets forth these spiritual requirements. Those who have not experienced the Spirit's regenerative work and cannot therefore measure up will be banished from the King's presence before He sets kingdom affairs in motion (Matthew 13:41; 24:51; 25:10,30).

The church saints, the Old Testament saints, and the tribulation martyrs will all have glorified bodies. All of these together will rule and reign with Christ over the earth for a thousand years (Revelation 20:4, II Timothy 2:12). The glorified saints will not make their residence on the millennial earth but will all live in the New Jerusalem. Some suggest the likelihood that this eternal city will circle earth as a satellite throughout the millennial age.

The glorified saints of all the former ages will rule over the earth, will have access to the earth, and will have social intercourse with the residents of earth (Matthew 8:11), but the proper home of the glorified saints is the city that lies four-square (Revelation 21:16). It may be that the unglorified saints on earth will have access to the New Jerusalem in space (Revelation 21:24-26; 22:14).

We can be fairly certain that at the beginning of the kingdom age not one unregenerate person will live in Palestine. All Jews will return from global dispersion, but unsaved Jews will get no farther than the border of the land, where the Lord will purge them out (Ezekiel 20:38). Only godly Jews will reside in Zion (Isaiah 4:3).

We can also be sure that not one unsaved Gentile will remain alive in Palestine. All of those Gentile nations who gather in the Middle East at the end of the tribulation period will meet their doom by the personal appearing of Christ. At that time He will divide the sheep (saved Gentiles) from the goats (unsaved Gentiles). The sheep will enter into the blessings of the millennial reign. They have the guarantee of eternal life. The goats will suffer eternal ruin. They will be barred from participation in the millennium and go away into everlasting punishment (Matthew 25:34-46).

It is possible that every unsaved Gentile on earth will be destroyed when Christ judges the Gentile nations in the Valley of Jehoshaphat. Or, possibly, Gentile peoples who are not present in Palestine and who do not participate in the military assault against Israel and against Christ will be spared destruction and will await evangelization. This seems to be the explanation for Isaiah 42:4: "He [Christ] shall not fail nor be discouraged, till he have set judgment [justice] in the earth; and the isles shall wait for his law."

The Messiah may very well gradually extend His dominion until all of the peoples of earth will own His rights and bow to His rule. Certainly Isaiah 9:7 implies some kind of progress in the extension of the millennial kingdom: "Of the increase of his government and peace there shall be no end." If His government extends equally and simultaneously to every remote recess of the planet, at the beginning of the millennium, then in what sense will that government increase?

However you explain the increase of Messiah's governmental authority, progress will be a feature of millennial rule. In a way, the postmillennialists are partially right—at least in their view of progress. But they err in thinking the church age and the gospel will produce the progress. They have their progress in the wrong age. It belongs to the millennial age, at which time God may indeed employ scientific technology, world evangelization, social agencies, and political platforms to execute the King's plans for a historical Utopia.

In making such a concession to the postmillennial view

of inevitable progress, however, we must be careful never to minimize the supernatural elements in the coming Messianic age. At the present time God manages His affairs on earth through providential agencies (Genesis 1:26, 28; Psalm 8:6-8). He executes His will for the most part by means of natural law or occasionally by means of divine interventions. But the kingdom age will be a time for many supernatural intrusions of power (Hebrews 6:5). The mighty works of the divine King will be visible and tangible. The peoples of earth will see the King in His beauty (Isaiah 33:17). They will hear of the wonders He performs. You can count on it, the age of the most stupendous miracles still lies ahead in human history.

THE SHOWDOWN . . .

13

The Affairs of
the Kingdom

The Affairs of the Kingdom

Are we told what the kingdom reign of Jesus Christ on earth will be like? Yes, the Bible gives us more details about life in the kingdom age than about any other subject. The material is abundant and plain. It covers the whole range of human activity.

Political affairs. The Messiah-King will exercise His regal authority through concrete forms and organization. He will introduce a system of government which will implement the principles He proposes. The body politic will reinforce the King's program. The government will have judicial, legislative, and executive powers all combined in the King (Isaiah 33:17,22). The functions of state will concentrate in the person of Christ. He will direct the affairs of state and provide a unifying center for its various activities.

When Christ sits upon the throne of Israel, He will fulfill the covenant promise to David in which God swore to establish David's throne and kingdom forever (II Samuel 7:13,16; Psalm 89:20-37). According to Gabriel's promise to Mary, Jesus will reign over the house of Jacob forever as the legitimate descendant of David (Luke 1:32,33).

This does not mean that Christ will sit continuously upon the throne in old Jerusalem or that He alone will govern the nations. That throne is certainly the symbol of His royal authority, and He will certainly sit upon it as occasion warrants. But His place of residence is not the old Jerusalem below but the New Jerusalem above, where the glorified dwell (Hebrews 12:22-24). Christ will act indeed as supreme head of state, but He will appoint princes and people to various positions of legislative and judicial authority.

We have already noted that the twelve apostles will sit upon twelve thrones judging the twelve tribes of Israel (Matthew 19:28). Daniel 7:22 predicts that judgment will be given to the saints of the Most High and that they will possess the kingdom. Isaiah 32:1 promises that princes will "rule in judgment."

Several passages of Scripture, such as Jeremiah 30:9, declare that King David will rise from the dead and rule in the kingdom. When Christ is bodily absent from the throne in Jerusalem, there is no reason why King David cannot assume responsibility for the affairs of state.

To the saints Christ will delegate various responsibilities. Some will rule over much; others will rule over little—all depending upon their faithfulness to Christ during the time of waiting for the kingdom age to begin (Luke 19:13,17-19).

Israel itself will be a ruling nation. It will rise to international political supremacy. Foreign kings will minister to Israel (Isaiah 49:23; 60:12-14). Gentile nations will contribute to Israel's economic prosperity (Isaiah 60:5-7,16,17). Israel's rule will guarantee the welfare of the nations.

Gentile kings will also rule over various principalities, countries, and nations (Revelation 21:24). Christ will be King over all the other kings and Lord over all the other lords. The millennial government will take the form of a theocratic hierarchy. The idea of a classless society is contrary to the whole millennial system.

The political kingdom is everlasting, not in the sense that history is eternal but in the sense that the King is an eternal person and also in the sense that no empire will ever destroy it or replace it (Daniel 7:14,18,27). At the end of the thousand years the mediatorial kingdom of history will merge into the universal kingdom of eternity. In a way, the millennial (mediatorial) kingdom is the vestibule of eternity, for the regenerate citizens of the kingdom will live as long as the kingdom endures and then enter into the eternal state (Matthew 25:46b).

A central authority will settle international disputes (Isaiah 2:4). A benevolent dictatorship will decide the behavior of the superpowers. The strategic location of Jerusalem at the crossroads of three continents and the sacred associations of the city with King David will make it a natural center of world politics and the capital city of the world.

Social affairs. At last, there will be social justice for all classes. The efficiency of the King's government will insure this. Christ will exercise a strict justice balanced by a gracious benevolence (Isaiah 11:3-5). No one will be able to deprive anyone else of his rights. Christ will guarantee and maintain the right of private ownership (Micah 4:4, Isaiah 65:21-23). Men will work and enjoy the fruits of their labors with no fear of exploitation. Work will acquire a new dignity and will arise from a new incentive. Welfare will be a thing of the past.

Men will turn their genius away from inventing weapons of destruction to inventing means for social progress (Isaiah 2:4). The nations will forget how to wage war. All military academies will shut down for the duration of the millennium. With the absence of war, violence, and crime, the population will phenomenally increase (Isaiah 9:3; Jeremiah 30:19), and yet the King will arrange for full employment and for economic prosperity.

Domestic tranquility and happiness will prevail. The King will restore the home and marriage to its pristine loveliness. Old people will sit once more on the street without fear of molestation (Zechariah 8:4,5). Boys and girls will frolic in the streets in joy and safety. Nothing will alarm the citizens of Messiah's kingdom.

Racial tensions will dissipate. Frantic outbursts of anti-Semitism will never again erupt. Arabs and Jews will live together in peace (Isaiah 11:13; 19:23-25). Minority groups will have no cause for resentment and redress. Social revolutions cannot disturb the all-pervasive calm. Every wrong will be righted. Slums and ghettos will disappear, with everything else that is ugly and wretched. Men will no longer waste earth's natural resources or spoil its natural beauty. The millennial kingdom will foster social progress without sacrificing a single citizen.

No barriers, such as diverse languages and cultures, will remain to cause misunderstanding and discord in the international community (Zephaniah 3:9). The nations will have no reason jealously to preserve their distinctive cultures at the expense of world peace.

Illiteracy and ignorance will vanish. The King will introduce sound educational principles. His servants will teach the nations His ways (Isaiah 2:3; 11:9; 32:4; 54:13). The earth will be full of the knowledge of the Lord.

Physical affairs. All sorts of physical, agricultural, topographical, and meteorological changes will accompany the establishment of the kingdom. The citizens of the kingdom will be free of deformity and disease (Isaiah 32:3,4; 35:5,6). The leaves on the tree of life in the heavenly Jerusalem evidently will maintain the health of the nations on earth (Revelation 22:2).

Occurrences of death during the millennium will be a rarity. Neither accident, disease, nor old age will be a cause of death. The charter citizens of the kingdom age will live throughout the 1,000-year period. It seems, however, that periodically a divine judgment will remove those sinners born during the millennium who do not trust the Saviour-King by the time they reach 100 years of age (Isaiah 65:20). The Lord will visit any outbreaks of rebellion against His government with immediate retribution.

Many of the circumstances that cause death—famine, war, catastrophe, birth defects, infection, travel accidents, industrial hazards—will be solved. Floods, lightning, tornados, and other "acts of God" will never occur. The divine King will directly control the elements (Isaiah 4:5,6).

The disturbances of weather cannot occur, for the King will introduce radical changes in the climate. Climatic alterations will contribute to the productivity of the land. Abundant rainfall will amply water the arid places of earth, making them fertile (Joel 2:21-24; Isaiah 35:1-7). Harvest will become so plentiful that at planting time the storehouses will still be full (Amos 9:13). Agriculture will not need to depend upon artificial irrigation, chemical fertilization, insecticides or pesticides.

Geological factors, as you know, are involved in climate. It is not surprising, then, to read about extensive topographical changes in the millennial age. For all we know, our present great mountain ranges will sink or at least diminish. During the tribulation the earth will reel to and fro (Isaiah 24:20). Unparalleled earthquakes will convulse the planet (Matthew 24:7; Revelation 11:13; 16:18). These will produce changes in the earth's surface.

Jerusalem will become a seaport (Zechariah 14:8) and the whole terrain around the city will undergo an uplifting (verse 10). In the process of these physical changes the waters of the Dead Sea will become so fresh it will become the favorite haunt of fishermen (Ezekiel 47:8-10).

The world of nature will undergo a dramatic transformation, as we see in Isaiah 11. Wild, predatory animals will lose their fierce and carnivorous nature. Lions will eat grass, not goats. Poisonous serpents will pose no threat even to a child who plays over their den. No harm of any sort can come to millennial saints. The King will supernaturally control the whole realm of nature to make the environment healthful and safe.

Nothing can be plainer than the fact that the millennial age is at least a partial return to the conditions of Eden before the tragic fall of Adam. During the millennium the King will partially lift the curse from nature. The natural world will reach a stage just short of perfection. It will not attain glorification during the millennium, but it will come close to it.

In that day sinners will not be able to lay the blame upon their environment, upon social evils, or even upon the devil. At the beginning of the kingdom age Christ will incarcerate

Satan in the bottomless pit for the duration of the millennium. There he cannot deceive or influence anyone. What excuse will the rebels give for defying the King, for spurning His grace, and for despising the precious blood of Jesus' cross?

Of course, they are utterly destitute of excuses. The glories of the King and the kingdom surround them. All nature serves them. They live in a holy society. And yet despite these unique privileges, some descendants of the charter citizens pay only lip service to Christ and bide their time to commit treason against His righteous government. How do you account for it?

Only one answer suffices: the heart is a rebel. A man's main problem is not his environment or even his heredity. He cannot usually plead, "The devil made me do it." Men will act sinfully no matter how perfect their environment, for man is essentially sinful. It is his fallen nature to be a rebel against God and His Christ. A perfect environment and the imprisonment of the devil does not change the basic flesh nature. Nor would a thousand years in jail alter man's nature, as the career of the devil pointedly illustrates.

Marvelous circumstances and wonderful privileges do not change the sinful human heart. These circumstances and privileges only increase the sinner's guilt for having sinned against so much light and goodness. Only the operations of almighty grace can change the human heart. It requires the same omnipotent energy to subdue the rebel heart as it requires to eliminate savagery from a wild brute.

Some who live for a while during the millennium will be strangers to God's great grace. Though they may succeed in suppressing their essential animosity to the King's holiness, eventually it will erupt, and the King will banish them from the millennial earth.

Moral affairs. The present moral declension in politics, education, and society is so widespread that thoughtful souls almost despair. Let us take heart; the King is coming.

He will reverse the downward trend. He will destroy those who ridicule moral standards and glorify lust. He will impose His own moral standards upon the millennial society. His standards will settle all questions of ethical right and wrong.

When Christ readjusts moral values, men will no longer call the wicked great or call evil good and good evil (Isaiah 32:5). Millennial citizens will call things by their right names. They will discern moral distinctions because they have benefited from the instructions of the King.

In the millennial age the King will permit no lies, no deceit, no fraud. Relative truth will give way to absolute truth. Situation ethics will cease. Immorality will terminate. The King will call a halt to every vice and put restraints upon every excess. The wicked will not prosper, as they do now.

The saints will not have to ponder over the seeming never-ending injustices or wonder why evil seems to triumph over the good. The King will honor moral uprightness. He will dispense instant retribution upon the violators of His moral law and will reward the faithful with immediate tokens of His pleasure (Psalm 72:4,7). He will resolve every moral contradiction to the satisfaction of His people.

Each individual person will bear the full consequences of his own moral actions. No child will ever again suffer because his father has sinned. Parents cannot then involve an unborn baby in future disasters because of their moral transgressions. Perfect justice will at last govern all human relations.

14

The Spirituality of the Kingdom

The Spirituality of the Kingdom

The coming kingdom of Christ is essentially spiritual. By noting its spiritual nature, you should not think of something invisible, intangible, or mystical. We do not mean that the kingdom is simply the exercise of God's bare sovereignty and authority over His creatures. In speaking of the spirituality of the kingdom, we mean that life in the politico-social kingdom of Messiah will be regulated according to spiritual principles.

We have already had occasion to discuss the fact that participation in the kingdom at the time of its inauguration requires the new birth. Regeneration is the price of admission to the kingdom age. This is the emphatic teaching of John 3:5.

All of the conditions which will prevail during the kingdom age are the outworking of the New Covenant. The New Covenant guarantees the nation Israel both spiritual and material blessings forever. The material blessings include a national regathering to Palestine, where the people will dwell permanently, a prodigious increase of produce, the reconstruction of their cities, the reclamation of barren land, and the enormous multiplication of population. (Ezekiel 36:24,28-30,33-38). The spiritual blessings include cleansing from sin, regeneration, the indwelling presence of the Spirit, and a hatred for sin (Ezekiel 36:25-27,29,31,33).

The Mosaic Covenant was incapable of securing for Israel the guarantees of the Abrahamic Covenant, the Palestinian Covenant, and the Davidic Covenant. The Mosiac Covenant could not make the people spiritual; it could only point out their utter sinfulness.

God intends to fulfill the covenant promises on a national scale to the spiritual descendants of Abraham, and so He introduced a covenant which will guarantee their national conversion and spiritual acceptability. This is the pledge of the New Covenant.

By the "spiritual descendants of Abraham" we do not mean the church, although the church is indeed a spiritual beneficiary of the Abrahamic blessings. We mean Abraham's physical descendants who are not numbered with the church saints but who receive forgiveness of sin and a new heart. The blood of Christ is the guarantee that God will fulfill all of the terms of the New Covenant to national Israel during the millennium.

The Israel of Jesus' day labored under the delusion that the law of Moses could make them acceptable before God. But for all of their scrupulous attention to the law, the nation as a whole was spiritually unfit for participation in the promised kingdom of Messiah. The setting up of the kingdom did not occur, as announced by Jesus, because the people for whom it was especially designed could not meet any of its spiritual demands.

When the Lord Jesus Christ returns, national Israel's spiritual state will be altogether different. The Lord will implement the terms of the New Covenant. A mighty outpouring of the Spirit of God upon the people will cause them to repent of their sins (Isaiah 32:15; 44:3; Zechariah 12:10-14). They will receive cleansing and regeneration. God will intervene in grace to save them spiritually.

The outpouring of the Spirit will also include the Gentiles (Joel 2:28,29). Only saved Gentiles will be admitted to Messiah's kingdom.

The residents in Jerusalem will be saved and sanctified; they will be holy. Holiness will characterize everything from the Temple to the cooking utensils in the kitchen (Isaiah 4:3; Zechariah 14:20,21).

The millennial saints will enjoy the imputed righteousness of Christ (Jeremiah 23:6). They will recognize Him to be "The Lord Our Righteousness." They will render to the

Lord the obedience that is His due (Deuteronomy 30:2,6,8).

The Holy Spirit will cause spiritual joy to well up in the millennial saints (Isaiah 61:2,3). He will impart to them His peace. The kingdom of God is righteousness, joy, and peace in the Holy Ghost (Romans 14:17). The saints will have spiritual understanding (Isaiah 54:13; Habakkuk 2:14). In short the Holy Spirit will produce the fruit of the Spirit in the millennial saints on a much grander scale than anything He now produces in church saints.

The millennial saints will give expression to their inward spirituality by observing external forms of worship. During the millennium religion and government will merge. Christ will sit upon David's throne as a king-priest (Zechariah 6:12,13). He is, as you know, a priest forever after the order of Melchisedek, who was also both a king and a priest (Psalm 110:4).

God called Israel to become a kingdom of priests (Exodus 19:6). The whole nation was to serve in a sacerdotal capacity. Israel will fulfill this destiny during the millennial age (Isaiah 61:6). Her religious functions will include teaching the Gentiles divine truth (Isaiah 43:8-10).

The city of Jerusalem will become the politico-religious capital of the world. From that city the Lord will promulgate His Word as well as His law (Isaiah 2:3). Delegates from every nation under the sun will visit Jerusalem once a year in order to engage in worship (Zechariah 14:16). The state will then enforce religious worship. Those nations that do not send representatives to Jerusalem will suffer drought and plague (Zechariah 14:17,18). The King will outlaw all religious dissent.

Worship will concentrate in a magnificent Temple. Solomon's temple, Zerubbabel's temple, and Herod's temple cannot compare with the millennial edifice. The Shekinah-glory will return to this Temple (Ezekiel 43:2-5; Haggai 2:7,9). The Lord will come suddenly to this Temple and sit there upon the throne of His glory (Malachi 3:1).

Ezekiel presents a full description of this Temple (chapters 40-44). No temple that ever existed in the past conforms to Ezekiel's dimensions. Conspicuous by their absence in the Millennial Temple are the ark, the mercy seat, the veil, the cherubim, and the tables of stone. A river flows from beneath the sanctuary south through a greatly enlarged Jerusalem and then divides to flow into the Dead Sea and the Mediterranean (Ezekiel 47:1-12).

Religious worship in the millennial age will include a sacrificial system. The prophets all speak of it (Ezekiel 43:19-27; Malachi 1:11). The institution of a priesthood and sacrifices does not mean a return to the Mosaic and Aaronic order. Although the millennial system resembles the Mosaic system in some respects, basic differences clearly distinguish them.

The priests who serve will derive from the sons of Zadok and not from the whole Levitical line (Ezekiel 44:15,16). The evening sacrifice will not be offered. Ezekiel makes no mention of the feast of Pentecost. The Day of Atonement will not be observed. The millennial sacrifices belong to an entirely new order; they are not a restoration of Judaism.

The millennial sacrifices do not relate to expiation at all; they are not intended to take away sin or to secure pardon for offenders of millennial law. The sacrifice of Christ provides the only expiation for sin (Hebrews 9:12,28; 10:10-12). The work at Calvary alone is efficacious. The millennial sacrifices have a memorial significance. They will serve as reminders to the millennial saints that kingdom provisions all rest upon the one offering of Christ at the cross.

In the daily blaze of Messiah's glory it would be easy for millennial citizens to forget that His sufferings and death provide the ground of continuing forgiveness and constitute the very basis of millennial splendor. The millennial sacrifices will permit no one to forget the significance of Calvary or the relationship of millennial conditions to the blood of the everlasting covenant.

These sacrifices may also serve to demonstrate the truths of salvation to the people who are born during the millennial age. Children growing up in the kingdom environment are responsible to receive Christ for themselves and rest their hope of salvation on the reconciling work of Christ. The sacrifices will serve to illustrate graphically and visually redemptive truth. Participation in the sacrificial rites will outwardly indicate that the offerer has already inwardly trusted Christ and relies upon the work of Calvary as the basis for his reconciliation to God.

It seems that the people who are born during the kingdom age will have 100 years to enter into cordial relations with Christ. If they fail to take advantage of their time of probation, they will meet a sudden judgment which will remove them from the millennial scene (Isaiah 65:20).

For a thousand years near-perfect conditions will prevail upon the earth. Satan will be bound in the abyss (Revelation 20:1-3). The Lord will periodically root sinners out of the millennial society. The millennial saints—both Jews and Gentiles—will experience such an absolute control of the Spirit they will probably never commit an act of sin (Ezekiel 36:27; 39:29; Joel 2:28,29). Although the saints will still possess their sinful nature, the Spirit's immeasurable fullness will prevent the sin nature from rearing its ugly head.

Christ will demonstrate that only a divine-human mediator is capable of managing world affairs. He will have His day of glory. He will be the object of universal adoration (Psalm 22:27,28; Isaiah 40:5; 66:23). God will thus vindicate His Son in the eyes of all mankind. He will bring history to a logical and glorious conclusion.

When the thousand years have run their destined course, God will release Satan from his prison house (Revelation 20:7,8). A thousand years in chains will restrict the devil's wicked inclinations. He will immediately launch a campaign to destroy the millennial saints and Jerusalem—the religious and governmental center of the Messiah.

Satan will appeal to the last generation of children born to millennial saints. Evidently thousands of these children will neglect the time of their probation by refusing to trust Christ as their Saviour. Satan will deceive them into thinking they are capable of vanquishing the King and overturning His kingdom of righteousness and holiness.

Perhaps under the guise of going to Jerusalem to worship at some annual feast, Satan will lead a countless number of sinners in an attack upon the capital city. Fire from Heaven will fall upon the rebel crowd, annihilating them (Revelation 20:9,10). The devil's final fling over, God will sentence him to everlasting torment in the lake of fire.

Then the final acts in history will take place. The millennial saints apparently will be glorified and removed from the earth. The New Jerusalem circling the earth will withdraw to a safe distance while the earth will undergo a global and atmospheric transformation. The earth will be purified by fire and gloriously renovated.

Meanwhile, out in space, Christ will preside at the Great White Throne judgment. He will empty Hades of its occupants and summon all of the wicked before Him (Revelation 20:11-13). He will review their works to decide upon the degree of severity for their endless punishment in Gehenna. This judgment will result in the banishment to Hell of every wicked being from the beginning of human history. In all likelihood apostate angels will be sentenced at the same time and to the same place. In the place of fire and brimstone the smoke of their torment will ascend forever and forever.

A complete renovation of earth will provide a place to accommodate the New Jerusalem. The eternal city will settle down upon the glorified and eternal earth (Revelation 21:1-3). Time will blend into eternity. The earth will be the eternal habitation of God and His saints—Old Testament saints, church saints, tribulation saints, and millennial saints. Christ will have delivered up the kingdom to the Father (I Corinthians 15:24). He will have relinquished His role as the mediatorial King of history. Throughout the everlasting eons of eternity the Father will "be all in all" (I Corinthians 15:28). And throughout the endless ages of eternity the Father will demonstrate to His glorified saints "the exceeding riches of His grace in his kindness toward us through Christ Jesus (Ephesians 2:7).

THE SHOWDOWN . . .

There remain some important questions for us as believers of the church age to consider and understand: What is the relationship of the church and the saints of the church age to the coming kingdom of Christ? What is our responsibility now toward the kingdom?

To begin with, we have already been translated into that kingdom before it actually dawns in history (Colossians 1:13). Through the new birth and the sanctifying influences of the Spirit, we are already qualified to participate in that kingdom as soon as it comes. In the same sense that we are now glorified, we are also in the kingdom. Our place in the kingdom is so certain God regards it as already accomplished.

We are praying for the kingdom to come, in harmony with our Lord's instructions to His disciples (Matthew 6:10). We are living with the kingdom in our sights (Matthew 6:33). We are laboring with the kingdom in view (Colossians 4:11). This does not mean we are laboring to bring in the kingdom through human effort, social agencies, or any other natural means. The kingdom will come suddenly and supernaturally by a divine intervention in history (Daniel 2:44,45; Luke 17:20).

We are looking forward to having an abundant entrance into that kingdom when it comes (II Peter 1:11). Meanwhile we realize that we must go through much tribulation before we enter the kingdom (Acts 14:22). The sufferings of the present are making us worthy to participate in that kingdom (II Thessalonians 1:5). We are continually engaged in teaching people about the coming kingdom and persuading people to believe on Christ that they might also share in His kingdom (Acts 19:8; 20:25; 28:23,31).

We believe that God is now delivering us from every evil work and preserving us so that we shall arrive safe and secure in the coming kingdom (II Timothy 4:18). We church saints are destined to be the King's consort. We are to be co-regents in that kingdom.

During the church age God is taking from Jews and Gentiles a special people (the bride of Christ) who will rule with Him and sit with Him upon His throne (Acts 15:14;

Revelation 3:21). Our future is all wrapped up in His glorious future. The millennial reign will provide the occasion for a full exhibition of Messiah's glory, and we saints of the church age will be partakers of that glory which shall yet be revealed.

May God hasten the day when the kingdoms of this world will become the kingdoms of our God and His Christ, and He shall reign forever and ever.

Be sure your trust is in the Saviour and coming King, and plan to enjoy the future reign of Christ on Planet Earth.